Dan Gartner

PE·METRICS™

Assessing National Standards 1-6 In Elementary School

Published by

National Association for
Sport and Physical Education
*an association of the American Alliance for Health,
Physical Education, Recreation and Dance*

NASPE Sets the Standard

1900 Association Drive, Reston, Va. 20191 (703) 476-3410 www.naspeinfo.org

© 2010, National Association for Sport and Physical Education,
an association of the American Alliance for Health, Physical Education, Recreation and Dance. All rights reserved.

PE Metrics™ is a trademark of the National Association for Sport and Physical Education, an association of the American Alliance for Health, Physical Education, Recreation and Dance.

To order more copies of this book (stock # 304-10494):

Web: www.naspeinfo.org
E-mail: customerservice@aahperd.org
Phone: (800) 321-0789; (412) 741-1288 outside the United States
Fax: (412) 741-0609
Mail: AAHPERD Publications Fulfillment Center, P.O. Box 1020, Sewickley, PA 15143-1020

ISBN: 978-0-88314-952-2

Printed in the United States

Acknowledgements

Assessment Task Force

Marybell Avery

Ben Dyson

Jennifer L. Fisette

Connie Fox

Marian Franck

Kim C. Graber

Judith H. Placek, chair

Judith Rink

Lori Williams

Weimo Zhu

Technical Assistance

Marco Boscolo

Connie Fox

Pamela MacFarlane

Youngsik Park

Weimo Zhu

NASPE Staff

De Raynes, Program Manager for Physical Education

Charlene Burgeson, Executive Director

Joe McGavin, Publications Manager

NASPE extends its appreciation to the many professionals who served as project administrators and coders in the gathering of thousands of pieces of individual student data for the Elementary Standard 1 assessments. This list includes: Ginger Aaron, Beverly Allen, Marybell Avery, Sherry Baggett-McMinn, Dominique Banville, Martie Bell, Debra Berkey, Carol Blair, Heidi Bohler, Mary Buddemeier, Eric Carpenter, Nancy Christensen, Catherine Conte, Mary Cramer, Judy Cunningham, Char Darst, Ben Dyson, Ellen Eisman, Joyce Ellis, Robert Emery, Heather Erwin, Matt Evans, John Ferguson, Hugh Ferry, Jennifer Fisette, Connie Fox, Marian Franck, Rodney Fry, Ovande Furtado, Ritchie Gabbei, Jere Gallagher, Caecilia Gropp, Mary Ann Guinn, Cindy Haigh, Tarin Hampton, Vanessa Hardbarger, Brent Heidron, Cindy Heos, Pat Hewitt, Lisa Hicks, Kathy Hixon, Kath Howarth, Becky Hull, Susan Jackson, Arcelia Jeffreys, Berniece Jones, Sherman Jones, Stephanie Jones, Pat Jordan, Susan Jordan, Michael Judd, Pam Keese, Barbi Kelley, Ulrike Kerstges, Kym Kirby, Tony Kirk, Gray Komich, Brenda Knitter, Toni Leo, Brenda Lichtman, Cindy Lins, Sue Long, Bob Martin, Carol Martini, Koji Matsushima, Marguerite McDonald, Shaunna McGhie, Chad McLarty, Doug McLerran, Beverly Nichols, Jamie O'Connor, Amber Phillips, Molly Pickering, Virginia Politano, Linda Poor, Penny Portman, Lisa Pryor, De Raynes, Suzanne Reed, Karen Roof, Patrice Scharin, Charlie Schmidt, Jan Scott, Eugenia Scott, Deborah Sheehey, Sally Smallwood, Kate Splendore, Susan Stewart, Marilyn Sting, Pat Stueck, Ann-Catherine Sullivan, Charmain Sutherland, Cetan Tameris, Sue Tarr, Jackie Thompson, Jen Thompson, Steve Underwood, Emily Vall, Julia Valley, Mindy Welch, Sharon Welch, Russ Williams, Carol Winckler, Nanette Wolford, Cheryl Wyatt.

In addition, NASPE extends its appreciation to more than 100 elementary physical educators, from all across the nation in every type of school and situation, who found time in their limited class hours to administer one or more of the Standards 2–6 cognitive tests. Their participation yielded thousands of student tests, which provided a rich source of data for establishing validity, reliability, item discrimination and other advanced data analysis applications.

Table of Contents

Introduction

Standards-Based Education

Since the late 1980s, education reform in the United States has been driven largely by setting academic standards that describe what students should know and be able to do, and developing accountability systems for measuring student achievement of those standards. Terms such as "standards-based education," "standards-based education reform" and "standards movement" are common in today's education vernacular.

Standards and assessment have been pivotal themes in recent reform efforts, cutting across much of the federal legislation that Congress has passed to improve education for all students. Standards-based education began in 1994, when Congress passed Goals 2000: The Educate America Act. That established a framework for identifying world-class academic standards, measuring student progress and providing support for any student needing help in meeting the standards. Goals 2000 codified eight national education goals:

1. School readiness.
2. School completion.
3. Student achievement & citizenship.
4. Teacher education & professional development.
5. Mathematics and science excellence.
6. Adult literacy & lifelong learning.
7. Alcohol- and drug-free schools.
8. Parental participation.

Since Goals 2000, Congress has amended and/or reauthorized the Elementary and Secondary School Education Act of 1965 (ESEA) twice. The 1994 ESEA reauthorization, dubbed the Improving America's Schools Act, focused on changing the way education is delivered, encouraging comprehensive school reform, upgrading instruction and professional development to align with high standards, strengthening accountability and promoting the coordination of resources to improve education for all children.

The most recent ESEA reauthorization, the No Child Left Behind Act of 2001 (NCLB), prescribes increased accountability for states, school districts and schools, greater choice for parents and students (particularly those attending low-performing schools), more flexibility for state and local education agencies in using federal education dollars and a stronger emphasis on reading, especially for the youngest children. Together, those federal laws have established many of the principles of standards-based reform, including the expectation that *all* students will attain high standards of academic excellence.

Standards-based education requires clear, measurable standards for all students. Standards and benchmarks identify what students should know and be able to do as they progress through school. They should be written so that they are developmentally appropriate and relevant to future education and employment needs. They also should be written so that all students are capable of achieving them, and so that talented students will exceed them.

Standards are meant to be anchors, aligning curriculum, instruction and assessment. That explains the emergence of the terms "standards-based curriculum," "standards-based instruction" and "standards-based assessment," as well as the holistic term "standards-based education." By design, standards-based education lends itself to accountability.

Standards-Based Accountability

In years past, education accountability was conducted by measuring school inputs and processes such as funding levels, curriculum offerings and resources and regulation compliance. After national and state standards emerged, policymakers began to shift the focus of accountability to student outcomes. Now, policymakers are emphasizing student learning and achievement outcomes to gauge the success of state and local education efforts. This trend in education reform is known as standards-based accountability. Systems have been and continue to be put into place to hold states, districts, schools and teachers accountable for the performance of their students.

Standards-based accountability systems use criterion-referenced performance standards rather than norm-referenced rankings. A standards-based system measures each student against the concrete standard, instead of measuring how well a student performs when compared to others.

Once standards are established, the next step in building a standards-based accountability system is aligning curriculum to the standards. The knowledge or skills that students must acquire to meet the standards must be defined, and criterion-referenced assessments must be established to determine the extent to which students meet the standards. The alignment of instruction and formative assessment of the standards must follow.

Standards-Based Education & Accountability for Physical Education

The National Association for Sport and Physical Education (NASPE) has established itself as a leader in standards-based education. In 1995, NASPE published *Moving Into the Future: National Standards for Physical Education*, followed by a second edition in 2004.

NASPE's National Standards for Physical Education state that "physical activity is critical to the development and maintenance of good health. The goal of physical education is to develop physically educated individuals who have the knowledge, skills and confidence to enjoy a lifetime of healthful physical activity" (NASPE, 2004). NASPE defines a physically educated person by these six standards.

1. Demonstrates competency in motor skills and movement patterns needed to perform a variety of physical activities.
2. Demonstrates understanding of movement concepts, principles, strategies and tactics as they apply to the learning and performance of physical activities.
3. Participates regularly in physical activity.
4. Achieves and maintains a health-enhancing level of physical fitness.
5. Exhibits responsible personal and social behavior that respects self and others in physical activity settings.
6. Values physical activity for health, enjoyment, challenge, self-expression and/or social interaction.

The national standards are presented in grade-level ranges representing grade ranges K-2, 3-5, 6-8 and 9-12, so that the ranges are consistent with children's and youths' developmental patterns, that they reflect organizational patterns in public school settings and that they align with other content areas. Each grade range contains two sections: student expectations and sample performance outcomes. Student expectations reflect what students should know and be able to do at the end of each grade-level range (e.g., K-2). Sample performance outcomes are examples of student behavior at each grade-level range that demonstrate progress toward meeting the standards.

Until now, nationally tested assessments and rubrics to measure student achievement of the national standards and benchmarks have been the missing elements of standards-based physical education. With its publication of PE Metrics, NASPE has closed the gap.

PE Metrics provides valid and reliable standards-based assessments and rubrics ("NASPE assessments") to measure student achievement of the national standards by high school graduation and appropriate progress at three other grade-level ranges. The book's assessments give evidence of learning through student work/performance, and its rubrics describe the quality of the work/performance. With PE Metrics, teachers and schools have the ability to report student progress on each standard. The advantage to that approach is that it provides students, teachers and parents with highly specific information.

It's critical to align curriculum, instruction and assessments with one another and with state and national standards. To provide students with a truly standards-based physical education, teachers must be certain that the material on which students are being assessed aligns with what's being taught in class.

Assessment as part of the instruction process constitutes much more than evaluation and accountability. Teachers should use a variety of techniques, including NASPE assessments, as part of regular classroom instruction. Assessment integrated with instruction (e.g., pre-assessment and formative assessment) is imperative for maximizing student learning and success. It's equally important to use pre-assessment and formative assessment to communicate important skills and knowledge to students and to prepare students properly for summative assessment.

For accountability purposes, it isn't necessary to assess all students on every task; one can use a random sample of student performance to guide curriculum development and/or to report on programmatic success to school, district and/or state leaders.

Whether PE Metrics assessments are used as part of the instruction process (e.g., pre-assessment and formative assessment) or for evaluation and accountability, they are scientifically valid and useful tools for measuring student achievement.

Overview of NASPE's PE Metrics Assessment Project

The National Association for Sport and Physical Education (NASPE) is committed to the tenets of high-quality physical education, which include the opportunity for all children to learn through supportive policies and environment (e.g., certified teachers, adequate facilities and equipment), national standards, high-quality curriculum, appropriate instruction practices, and student and program assessment. NASPE continues to develop tools to help schools, districts and states implement assessments that measure student progress toward state and national physical education standards. As the only national association for physical education, NASPE feels a strong obligation to develop valid and reliable assessments that teachers throughout the nation can use.

In March 1999, NASPE assembled a "think tank" of university and public school professionals to consider how to best advance K-12 physical education. The group was charged with recommending a plan of action to confront the barriers to high-quality physical education. The priority recommendation was to develop performance indicators and practical assessments to evaluate student progress toward the National Standards for Physical Education.

In January 2000, NASPE created what became known as its Assessment Task Force, made up of curriculum and instruction and measurement and evaluation experts, researchers, teacher educators, K-12 physical education teachers, administrators and students. NASPE charged the task force with developing performance indicators that corresponded to the national standards at each grade-level range (K-2, 3-5, 6-8 and 9-12), as well as assessments for each indicator. The performance indicators were not meant to be a comprehensive set of all possible skills and knowledge that students should master in a specific grade-level range, but rather samples of performance outcomes that could be expected within that grade-level range.

Performance Indicator & Assessment Development

Just as it was not feasible to identify all possible performance indicators, it became clear to the task force that it would not be feasible to write all possible assessments for each indicator. Ultimately, the task force identified a broad range of performance indicators and wrote a variety of assessments to measure student skills and knowledge. The examples selected and presented in this book and CD-ROM provide templates of good assessments that can serve to guide teachers, districts and states in developing additional assessments.

Standard 1

Initially, task force members were paired with content experts, and writing the assessments occurred over a period of many years. The draft performance indicators and assessments that they developed were introduced to 220 professionals attending a session at the 2001 American Alliance for Health, Physical Education, Recreation and Dance (AAHPERD) National Convention. NASPE continued to update the indicators and assessments and to solicit member feedback during AAHPERD National Conventions each year, as well as at other state and regional conferences.

Standards 2-6

Once the Standard 1 assessments were written and in the process of being pilot-tested, the task force focused on developing assessments for Standards 2-6. After writing performance indicators, the task force originally developed a series of authentic assessments for Standards 2-6. As early drafts of the assessments were tested, however, it became clear that the task force would not be able to develop authentic assessments (e.g., determining student ability to cooperate in class) that were reliable and valid. Therefore, the task force decided to use written tests (true/false, multiple-choice) to measure learning outcomes for Standards 2-6. These tests were written by small committees of content experts, under the direction of task force members

The test-writing committees developed tables of specifications to ensure that the questions were written at the appropriate level of difficulty and reading comprehension and were linked to the content within each performance indicator. Rather than developing five separate tests (one for each standard), the committees grouped the questions into three broad concept areas (Standard 2; Standards 3 & 4; and Standards 5 & 6). The committees wrote three forms of each grade-level test (A, B & C) for each concept area, with 30 true/false questions for grade 2 and 40 multiple-choice questions for grade 5. No written assessments were developed for kindergarten students because committee members believe that a written test is not appropriate for that grade level.

Institutional Review Board Approval

In preparing for the data collection, NASPE obtained Institutional Review Board (IRB) approval for using human subjects in a research study from the University of Illinois at Urbana-Champaign (UIUC) and Northern Illinois University (NIU). NASPE obtained IRB approval in 2003, and it has been renewed each year. Although the IRB document was written to enable project administrators from different universities to use the same consent documents, the project administrators were advised to make sure that UIUC's IRB approval would satisfy the IRB requirements at their home institution. In the end, all project administrators submitted joint agreements with UIUC or were covered under NIU's IRB. An additional IRB was obtained from NIU for administering Standards 2-6 tests.

Data Collectors
Standard 1

NASPE trained teacher educators to supervise the administration of the pilot and national data collection for Standard 1. These project administrators were chosen based on four criteria:
1. They had established contacts with teachers and administrators in the public schools through their placements of pre-service students for field experience.
2. They had experience with video-recording student performances.
3. They had knowledge of the appropriate execution of motor skills.
4. Their research backgrounds meant that they understood the importance of adhering strictly to testing protocols, including obtaining school district permission and parent/student consent for testing, as well as following the exact assessment description and instructions, including equipment, site preparation, safety and video-recording.

Project administrators were recruited through personal contacts made by NASPE staff and task force members. They received six hours of training that included a project history and overview, roles and responsibilities (including gaining entry, informed consent, video-recording and coding), protocols for video-recording and conducting the assessments, typical video-recording problems and guidelines for coding the video records. Training took place at AAHPERD National Conventions (2004, 2005, 2006 & 2007) and at regional and district conferences (2004, 2007).

Standards 2-6
Task force members and NASPE staff recruited elementary physical education teachers from around the

country to administer the tests to their students. The tests, detailed instructions and Scantron answer sheets were sent to the teachers and subsequently returned to the researcher at NIU for initial analysis. In addition to administering the tests, teachers were asked to review questions for content and readability and to provide feedback to the task force.

Process for Testing & Data Collection

Standard 1 assessments and Standards 2-6 written tests were subjected to the following sequence of testing:

- Pre-pilot data collection.
- Pilot data collection.
- National data collection.

Because Standard 1 measures skill performance, testing involved video-recording each assessment, then coding the videos to produce scores for each aspect of the students' performance. Because of the seasonal nature of instruction in physical education (e.g., restrictions imposed by inclement weather), pilot and national data collection took longer than anticipated. Because Standards 2-6 assessments are paper-and-pencil tests that measure students' cognitive knowledge, they were easier to administer, required fewer personnel and were completed more quickly than the Standard 1 assessments.

Pre-Pilot Data Collection

Standard 1

All assessments were pre-piloted by at least one elementary teacher and 20 students. Teachers provided feedback on the instructions to teachers and students, camera placement and level of difficulty for the assessment task. The task force revised the assessments based on that feedback, as well as on feedback obtained during AAHPERD National Convention sessions. During the pre-pilot phase, NASPE reduced the number of National Standards from seven to six. As a result, the task force modified both the performance indicators and assessments to meet the new standards and grade-level ranges. Accordingly, the task force collected additional data and pre-pilot feedback for some of the Standard 1 assessments.

Standards 2-6

Three forms of each test at each grade level were administered to a minimum of 20 students in December 2008, and teachers provided feedback on readability, clarity and ease of administration. The task force revised questions based on teacher feedback and on conventional data analysis (item difficulty and discrimination). Based on the analysis, the task force identified the strongest questions, which were used as common questions on each form of the three tests (A, B & C) to be used for pilot testing (five common questions for grade 2; 10 common questions for grade 5).

Pilot Data Collection

Standard 1

Project administrators subsequently tested the assessments on a larger scale to further ensure their appropriateness and to collect preliminary data on discrimination validity and reliability. The task force collected data from various sections of the country through an extensive network of project administrators. At least 40 students completed each pilot assessment. Project administrators collected parent/student/teacher consent forms, worked with an elementary physical education teacher to administer the assessments and video-recorded, coded and provided feedback on the assessments. The data were analyzed to ensure that the assessments were appropriately difficult and that they revealed meaningful differences among students. The task force revised the assessments as needed, based on data analysis and the feedback from teachers and project administrators.

Standards 2-6

The task force and NASPE staff recruited teachers from around the United States at AAHPERD and district conventions and from personal contacts to conduct one or more cognitive assessments, and 200 students completed each of the three forms of the Standards 2-6 test in January and February 2009. Data analysis identified a problem with discrimination and difficulty levels with a number of questions, so the task force revised the problematic questions. All the questions were pilot-tested again in October 2009 with a smaller number of students. The resulting data were analyzed, and the best questions were used to create two forms (A & B) of the test for each grade level for the national data collection.

National Data Collection

Standard 1

Data collection for the Standard 1 assessments began in February 2005 and continued through winter 2007-2008. (The IRB approval from UIUC continued to cover national data collection.) NASPE requested an additional IRB, which NIU approved during 2007 and 2008 to cover a subset of data collectors not named originally in the UIUC IRB. (See Table 1 on p. 24 for the list of assessments for which national data were collected.)

The project administrators' goal was to collect data from a minimum of 200 students for every assessment task. Two common tasks of medium difficulty were identified at each grade-level range, and all students at each grade-level range completed at least one of the two common tasks. The common tasks for Standard 1 elementary assessments were:

- Kindergarten: Hopping and Dribble With Hand.
- Grade 2: Dribble & Jog and Jump Forward.
- Grade 5: Soccer Dribble, Pass and Receive, and Strike With a Paddle.

The data from the common tasks were used in the research process to allow scores to be placed on a common scale. A common scale is important in being able to equate assessments across and within grade-level ranges and to create an assessment bank. These topics are explored further in the Psychometric Quality of Assessments chapter.

Standards 2-6

National data collection occurred in November and December 2009, with 400 students completing each form of the test (A & B) at each grade level (2 and 5). Data analysis was conducted in January 2010.

Summary

NASPE's Assessment Task Force has followed a long and difficult path in creating the PE Metrics assessments. In all, the process took more than 10 years of concerted, ongoing effort by the entire task force. Task force members believe that this careful and extensive process has resulted in valid and reliable assessments that are useful for teachers, administrators, teacher educators and researchers in both physical education and the wider field of education in general. The task force views its work as a first step in NASPE's ongoing effort to create and then add to a body of assessments for our field.

Using PE Metrics Assessments

In today's education climate, there's no place in the school curriculum for a program area that can neither define the outcomes that students should achieve nor measure the extent to which they have met those outcomes. Too many physical education programs have largely avoided doing both. The instruction process is said to be one of planning or defining outcomes, teaching so that students achieve those outcomes and assessing the extent to which students have mastered those outcomes. Too often, physical educators have felt that assessment "takes time away from instruction," and they have failed to recognize that assessment is a critical part of effective instruction.

The National Standards for Physical Education provide a guide for determining the critical outcomes of physical education. The standards are exit outcomes for the K–12 program. Effective physical education programs must measure student performance at particular grade levels en route to attaining the standards. The PE Metrics assessment materials provide grade-level performance indicators and related assessments that are valid and reliable measures to help with this process.

The assessment materials in this book were not designed to measure all program outcomes related to the standards but rather to identify critical outcomes in specific content areas at particular grade levels. They are not a "test" but rather a resource of assessment materials that teachers and administrators can put together to meet the needs of particular programs. Assessment materials should match what is taught in a program. Professionals at all levels are encouraged to select the assessments that are appropriate for their programs' goals.

Using the Assessments in This Book

The assessment materials in this book, in the accompanying CD-ROM and on the PE Metrics Web site, www.PEMetrics.org, are intended for use at different levels for a variety of purposes. Teachers; schools; school district administrators; local, state and national policymakers; and researchers will find them useful in different ways.

Teachers

The PE Metrics program is a total package that provides teachers with assessment materials that they can use in a variety of ways. It's also a package that provides teachers with a way to interpret assessment data and to report data.

Using PE Metrics for Formative & Summative Assessment

Teachers use both formative and summative assessment as part of the instruction process. The assessment materials in this book facilitate both types of assessment. Standard 1 (motor skills) is measured using observation rubrics that will be useful for both formative and summative assessment. Standards 2–6 assessments are written test items — provided both in the book in print form and on the accompanying CD-ROM — which will be more appropriate for summative assessment to determine Standards 2–6 knowledge.

Formative assessment helps teachers determine students' skill levels before and during the instruction phase. It's easy for teachers to make inaccurate assumptions about students' abilities when planning a unit of instruction, so testing them before planning the unit can make instruction far more appropriate.

Assessing students before planning a unit allows teachers to compare the results of assessment conducted prior to the unit with that conducted at the end of the unit (summative assessment). This practice — often referred to as pre- and post-assessment — facilitates teachers' ability to determine how much students have learned from instruction. Teachers can use the Standard 1 rubrics in this book to pre- and post-test students. They also can consider selecting items from the Standards 2–6 test bank provided on the CD-ROM as a pretest of what a student knows at the beginning of the school year.

Teachers also can use the Standard 1 rubrics to track students' performance over time, and to help students track their own performance. The newest motivation theories stress the importance of assessing students on their improvement over time and establishing learning climates that are mastery-oriented (students work for personal improvement) rather than ego-oriented (students are focused on comparing themselves to others). Assessment data can help students set appropriate goals and track progress toward those goals. Using self-assessment or peer assessment during the instruction process can motivate students to do well and helps provide students with a clear understanding of performance expectations, particularly when used in conjunction with personal goal-setting.

Summative assessment helps teachers identify how much students have learned as a result of instruction. Summative assessment occurs at the end of the instruction process. Valid and reliable assessment tools are critical to summative assessment. Teachers should use valid and reliable assessments to determine the effectiveness of instruction and student grades. Reports sent to parents and policymakers on student achievement should be based on objective data. The PE Metrics assessments are ideally suited for these purposes, because they're targeted toward the outcomes of instruction that is appropriate for different grade-level ranges.

Sampling Students to Collect Assessment Data

The PE Metrics Standard 1 assessments were designed so that each assessment has a difficulty level. This means that teachers can give different assessments to different students and actually equate the performance between the students. They also can assess different classes of the same grade on different assessments, compare scores and not have to assess every class on every assessment.

Grading

The primary purpose of PE Metrics is *not* to determine part of a student's grade. We understand, however, that teachers need a valid and reliable set of tools to calculate grades. The Standard 1 assessments in this book use a four-point rubric, and some readers might be tempted to transpose those scores as a four-point grade scale, in which 4 = A, 3 = B, etc. That is an inappropriate use of this tool. Instead, teachers must calculate students' grades by using their school's or district's grading policy.

Ideally, teachers will construct grades to reflect students' achievement of learning objectives. Certainly, developing skills, strategies and abilities in games and activities; achieving fitness; and enhancing personal and social responsibility are goals of most physical education programs, and grades reflecting students' achievement of objectives related to those goals are appropriate.

Teachers might have specific learning objectives that reflect tasks measured by the PE Metrics assessments. It's reasonable to state learning objectives for students to be able to jump and land, and to show skill in basketball offense, for example. Teachers must remember, however, that the purpose of the PE Metrics

Standard 1 assessments is to assess competence within Standard 1. Grades include many factors, some of which are not related to competence within Standard 1. Jumping and landing is not a goal, but it's an objective that will lead to the goal of competence within Standard 1.

Teachers can consider achievement of standards when grading, but that information is used more appropriately at a classroom, school or district level, announced as a percentage of students who have achieved the standard.

Reports to Parents

Using PE Metrics will allow teachers to compile data in different forms and send reports on student achievement to parents and guardians with suggestions for how they can help their children improve.

Teacher Preparation for Using PE Metrics Materials

Although teachers can use PE Metrics both formally and informally, the materials were designed as formal assessments. This means that if teachers want to compare student scores, the assessments have to be conducted according to the protocols provided. That's sometimes difficult for teachers who might want to improvise the space or equipment used, or who want to coach students differently about how to complete an assessment. To use the materials in this book appropriately, teachers must attend to the protocols provided, which requires preparation. That involves learning how to administer the test items and how to score them, which is explored in the next chapter.

District Administrators

PE Metrics assessment materials have many potential uses at the school district level. A district can more effectively help students meet physical education standards by graduation if it uses assessment data to track students' progress as they move through the K–12 program. For example, elementary, middle and high school programs can become better aligned with one another, and districts can standardize expectations for students across grades and schools. Used that way, assessment can help districts improve their curriculum planning.

Many physical education programs have functioned without accountability for student learning because there has been no systematic way to measure teacher effectiveness and little effort to measure student performance. Accountability does not limit good programs and teachers; rather, it enhances them. With accountability systems in place, schools can provide students with feedback on their level of performance and learning, and can provide parents with information about their children's progress. Assessment data allow schools and districts to track student achievement, evaluate curriculum needs and promote program improvement.

Districts don't need assessment data on each student to evaluate programs. Classes can be sampled to provide a measure of program assessment. Because NASPE developed PE Metrics assessments with a difficulty score for each assessment, districts can compare schools using different assessments.

Through assessment and accountability, physical education takes its place as a critical part of the overall school program. On the other hand, a lack of accountability can protect poor programs and ineffective teachers. Districts will find valid and reliable assessments essential to conducting high-quality physical education programs that produce graduates who value physical activity and have the knowledge and skills to be physically active adults.

Local, State & National Policymakers

Consciously or subconsciously, physical educators often overstate what their programs do for students. The field of physical education has claimed much but provided little evidence that it can deliver on these promises to students. Policymakers at all levels want to know whether the resources they pour into any program have any impact on students. Physical education programs in some areas of the country have been "cut" recently to provide more time for other academic subjects. Without valid assessment data, it is difficult to advocate that physical education programs can exert an impact on both the traditional goals of our programs and current national health problems.

With PE Metrics assessment materials, though, policymakers will have tools to determine the impact of physical education programs, assess student knowledge and skills in terms of program goals, track student progress over time, compare program quality across districts and states, and provide a way to hold teachers, schools, districts and states responsible for assessing outcomes and meeting program goals.

Researchers

Research on curriculum and instruction in physical education has been hampered by a lack of valid and reliable tools to assess student outcomes. A considerable amount of the research conducted on teaching, teachers and curriculum in physical education has been related to the processes of teaching without attending to the products of those processes. It's critical that the physical education profession be able to identify how to provide students with the skills, knowledge and dispositions they need to lead a physically active lifestyle. Evidence-based practice depends on good research, and good research depends on having a valid and reliable way to measure student achievement.

Valid outcome measures enable us to answer these questions:

- To what extent are the National Standards being achieved?
- Are students who achieve more related to the National Standards more physically active than those who achieve less?
- What curricula are most effective in helping students to achieve the national standards, and under what conditions for what outcomes?
- How do the standards relate to one another? For example, what is the relationship of skill in movement forms to participation in physical activity and fitness levels? How do we instruct students effectively to meet the outcomes we target?
- How are good physical education programs related to academic achievement?

The answers to those questions depend on having good measures of student performance. The PE Metrics assessment materials provide a foundation for measurement, data collection over time and accountability.

Misusing Assessment

Although assessment is a powerful tool for improving instruction and learning, it carries the potential for unintended and negative consequences. Assessment is being misused when:

- Students are assessed on concepts and skills that they haven't been taught or haven't been given enough time to learn.

- What's being assessed becomes the whole curriculum rather than a measured sample of what students should be learning as a part of a comprehensive curriculum.
- Scores that students receive on assessments are used exclusively to evaluate students, teachers, schools, districts or states.
- Using raw scores from a rubric as student grades.

While the PE Metrics assessments target critical outcomes that all students should achieve, they are not the only important outcomes of a good program. The ultimate goal in PE Metrics is to improve the quality of physical education programs. The assessment materials in this book can provide teachers, students, parents, administrators and policymakers with both formative and summative data. That information helps teachers improve instruction and demonstrate student learning. Administrators and policymakers also can use the data to determine the impact of physical education programs and, subsequently, to support those programs.

Procedures Used to Administer & Score PE Metrics Assessments

Standard 1

As part of the research procedures for this project, NASPE's Assessment Task Force collected data according to a rubric connected to each Standard 1 assessment. All student performances were video-recorded to facilitate data analysis, which included intra- and inter-rater reliability coding for data collection. Thousands of students participated in the national sample and provided data. The results of the coding enabled the task force to improve the quality and clarity of individual assessments and determine the most effective testing protocols.

For teachers using the PE Metrics assessments, video-recording allows them to view student performance on more than one occasion. It also enables greater scoring accuracy, because teachers can conduct an "instant replay" of an assessment by simply rewinding all or part of the record. Video-recording also provides teachers with hard evidence for documenting student achievement. Finally, video records provide a mechanism for teachers to conduct periodic self-checks of their scoring reliability.

The next section of this book contains procedures and directions for administering the assessments. The procedures and directions guide standardized administration of the assessments. Teachers who are conducting summative assessments must follow the protocols in each assessment precisely so that they can compare performances later, pre- and post-test, class to class, year to year, teacher to teacher or school to school. Before using the assessments (with the exception of pre-assessment), teachers should ensure that students have been taught the task and have had numerous opportunities to practice the skills exactly as described in the assessment.

Remember: Follow school or district guidelines regarding permission to record student performances.

Procedures for Administering the Assessments & Collecting Data
Administering the Assessments

Standard 1
Preparation

1. Prepare the score sheets ahead of time and have pencils, clipboard, stopwatch and other activity equipment required for the assessment on site.
2. Prepare all equipment (and perhaps some spare equipment) before the class enters the assessment setting. This should include taping mats, inflating balls, distributing safety mats and removing objects/equipment from around the perimeter of the space.
3. Prepare numbers and have safety pins or numbered pinnies/vests available prior to class. Make numbers as large as possible (10 inches high is suggested) in a color that contrasts with the shirt or pinnie/vest.
4. Assign numbers to students before class begins. Once students enter class, attach the numbers to students' fronts and/or backs, depending on the assessment. Students must be easily identifiable by number throughout the assessment.

5. Don't give two students in one class the same number. If you're recording on multiple days or for multiple assessments, students should maintain their numbers. If a student is absent, don't reassign that number.

6. When the assessment includes an offense and defense situation, provide students with different-color pinnies/vests to differentiate offense from defense.

7. Prepare alternative activities for students who are not involved in the assessments. Ensure that they're active, supervised and safe.

8. Once the testing area is identified and marked, set up the camera and record a trial run of the assessment before class to ensure that the viewfinder can "see" all essential elements of the entire assessment.

Video-Recording

1. When movement in rhythm to an accompaniment is part of the assessment, place camera and music source (if used) close together so that you can hear the music later, when reviewing the video record.

2. Camera set-up directions for each assessment are provided in the individual assessments. Follow them for each assessment unless your testing situation requires a different set-up. Ultimately, you must be able to see the entire activity area needed for an assessment, the trajectory or path of the ball or implement, the target when indicated, and the student's entire body (e.g., feet, head, number). That might require moving some cameras back farther if they don't have wide-angle lenses. It also might require adjusting the angle for the situation.

Safety Considerations

1. The court or floor surface should be dry, clean and clear of obstacles surrounding and beyond the boundary of the test area. Adequate out-of-bounds space is important for deceleration and turning, etc.

2. If you're testing outdoors, ensure that the surface is appropriate. A hard surface should be dry, smooth and clean. If the assessment calls for a grassy area, it should be mowed and free of grass clippings, hazards, trash, holes and obstructions.

3. Allow only safe footwear; no sandals, boots or bare feet.

4. Ensure that students know the testing area boundaries, that they understand the markings, are aware of the deceleration or stopping zone, and are clear about their personal space.

5. Set up the testing area so that other students can't enter it inadvertently.

6. Have students performing the assessment face away from distractions during testing.

7. Have students empty their pockets, remove jewelry, tie their shoes and take off accessories that might injure them or a partner. This is especially important for assessments that require rolling or inverted positions and/or performance with or against another person.

Warm-Up & Practice

1. A warm-up and short practice period is recommended. The assessments shouldn't be a secret; students should have had adequate learning time in previous lessons.

2. Provide students with adequate time to perform routines that have been created previously and written down, but don't allow them to read the routines during the assessment, and don't read the routine to the students. Also, don't recite directions to a dance during the assessment, and don't use music that has the directions on it.

Test Administration

1. As noted above, follow the camera set-up and placement directions for each assessment.

2. If possible, have a teacher administer the assessment and have another person record the performance.

3. Read "Directions to Students" exactly as they're written, so that the directions are audible to the students and on the video recording.

4. Be sure that all students understand the directions. Read them to small groups of students immediately prior to assessments for kindergarten and Grade 2, and to the entire class for Grade 5. In the latter instance, teachers might need to reread the instructions periodically if a long period of time elapses after having read them initially. Be fair; if it makes sense to read the instructions again for a student, do so.

5. Don't permit other students to act as an audience for those being assessed; make arrangements for others to be physically active and adequately supervised.

6. Ensure that the order of the students on the code sheet matches the order of the students on the video record. Record student names and numbers as seen on the video on the code sheet.

7. If feasible, have each student say his/her number in front of the camera in a loud voice immediately before beginning the assessment. Ask each student to stand 5 feet (sufficient distance to see the student's number and body) in front of the camera and state his/her name and number clearly. Alternatively, the assistant recording the assessment could say the student's name and number.

8. Use a "Ready/Start" signal to begin the assessment.

9. When an assessment requires using first one foot and then the other, or moving to the left and then right, or an out and return, instruct students to wait until you give them the signal to begin the second half of the assessment, the return, or the change of feet/hand. Pause before indicating "Start."

10. Be sure that students know what to do if action stops, whether they can restart and what to do if the ball goes far out of bounds. Also, be sure that they:

    a. Understand the important elements of an assessment (e.g., they might think that speed is the critical element, when the critical elements are accurate passes and controlling receptions).

    b. Understand the difference between a jog and a walk.

    c. Understand that they should resume an interrupted skill during a timed assessment.

    d. Know that trials that don't make it past a certain line or height won't count in the total but that they can keep going and try to resume the correct distance/height until time is up.

Coding Protocols

Study the assessment

1. Read the entire assessment carefully.

2. Study the major focus of each criterion.

3. Study the value difference of each level for all criteria, noting that Level 3 equals competence.

Preview/view the video record before trying to score

1. Look for the major focus of each criterion (practice for recognition of each).

2. Look for the differences in performance in relation to the quality level of each criterion (range of proficiency among performers; common errors).

3. Become familiar with the requirements of the criteria and corresponding performance levels of the assessments. Some Level 4 criteria use the term "fluid motion." This term was chosen to separate Level 4 from Level 3 performers by emphasizing the performance's flowing, smooth and graceful nature. A Level 4 performance should be effortless, refined and performed without hesitation. Typically, only a very small number of students in each class will be able to demonstrate a Level 4 performance.

Practice Scoring

1. View the first performer and make a decision about the first criterion and then all of the other criteria.
2. View as many times as necessary until you can determine a score consistently on each viewing.
3. Focus on one student at a time when the performance includes multiple students (dance, game situations), repeating the above steps for each.
4. Repeat until all students in the performance have been scored on all criteria.

Scoring (Use score sheet designed for each assessment)

1. Record student number and gender.
2. Record scores for all criteria and trials and for all students, as the assessment requires.
3. Total the scores for all criteria and record them on the score sheet in the designated column.
4. Repeat steps above for all performers on the video record.

Scoring Sheet Information

1. Fill out all of the scoring sheets for future use.
2. Write the school name and location on the cover of the DVD and on the DVD itself (to prevent confusion if the cover becomes separated from the DVD).

Standards 2-6

Administering the Standards 2-6 assessments is considerably easier than administering the Standard 1 assessments, because they're written true/false or multiple-choice tests. Administer and score the tests as you would any written test. Find a quiet place and provide students with pencils and the test forms. If possible, use a classroom, so that students can use desks. Read the questions and answer choices to grade 2 students, and to grade 5 students, as well, if necessary.

This book and the accompanying CD-ROM provide the questions, divided by performance descriptor so that you can select questions based on the content you've taught the students. If you want to assess only a few weeks' worth of instruction, five questions might cover the material. If you are assessing a larger amount of content, you can select more questions. The questions on the CD-ROM are ready for you to cut and paste into a test for students. The answer key is at the end of the questions. In the printed version of the test questions in this book, the correct answers are in **bold** type.

Psychometric Quality of Assessments

The assessments developed based on the National Standards for Physical Education must be psychometrically sound to make valid and reliable inferences of a student's ability. This chapter first provides a brief description of some key measurement concepts and theories employed in the PE Metrics project; namely, an assessment bank, item response theory and test equating. The chapter then describes calibrations of the assessments for Standards 1 and 2-6. Calibration is a process that sets assessment tasks on a common measurement scale and determines their psychometric quality.

New Concepts, Theory & Techniques Employed

Assessment Bank

In addition to publishing the assessment materials in book form, NASPE is developing an online physical education assessment bank: a collection of assessments of a variety of tasks that share the same scale that teachers will be able to access easily to select tasks tailored to a specific group (Umar, 1997). In other words, the assessment bank will include assessments ranked for difficulty and will allow teachers to select appropriately difficult tasks for a student or class of students.

Building an assessment bank depends heavily on two major new advances in modern assessment practice:

1. Item response theory (IRT).
2. Test equating.

Item Response Theory (IRT)

IRT was developed during the 1950s and 1960s in education measurement practice. Its relatively slow development accelerated in the 1980s due to the growing accessibility of personal computers and development of application software. Today, IRT is the most dominant theory for test construction within all major testing organizations and agencies. When compared to measurement models based on the Classical Testing Theory (CTT), which has been the primary testing theory in the field of physical education, models based upon IRT have several advantages (Hambleton, Swaminathan & Rogers, 1991; Spray, 1987). The primary advantages of IRT are that item parameters are independent of the ability level of the examinees responding to the items; and, at the same time, the ability parameters are independent of the items used in tests and the performance of other examinees. This is known as IRT's "invariance" feature. That is, the assessment item is not tied to the ability of the student, and the students are not bound to the difficulty of the test. Because of that feature, interpreting item difficulty and examinee ability is consistent in IRT. For example, a difficult item won't become easier when it's applied to a group of examinees with higher abilities.

Another important advantage of IRT is that item difficulty and student ability are set on the same scale, which makes it much easier to determine the appropriateness of an item for a given ability level and to interpret test scores. As a result, a teacher can select an assessment that is appropriately difficult for a student and can explain what the student's score really means. IRT has been used in physical education for many years and has been well-tested for its measurement advantages (see Safrit, Zhu, Costa & Zhang, 1992; Spray, 1987; Zhu, 1996, 2006; Zhu & Cole, 1996; Zhu & Safrit, 1993, for more information).

Test Equating

Test equating is a statistical procedure used to establish the relationship between scores from two or more tests or to place them on a common scale. The task of equating, in general, is to establish statistically a conversion relationship among summary scores from two or more test forms or tests. The relationship could be linear or non-linear, depending on the equating method employed. Test-equating methods, according to the test theory on which they are based, generally can be classified into two categories: traditional and IRT (Kolen & Brennan, 2004; Zhu, 1998). With test equating, putting two or more tests on the same scale becomes possible, which is also necessary for establishing an item or assessment bank. A number of successful test-equating applications in fitness testing based upon traditional equating approaches have been reported (Zhu, 1998, 2001). As a result, teachers can select any one assessment and will be able to anticipate a student's performance accurately on a different and dissimilar assessment. In this case, test equating will allow a comparison between a group of students' abilities in a basketball unit with a different group of students' ability in a soccer unit.

An assessment bank can provide several assessment advantages for teachers and data collectors. First, because the tasks are set on the same scale, testing scores generated will be equivalent to each other even when a different task is assessed. That allows cross-school comparison even when different tasks are used. In the past, cross-school comparisons often were established by using raw scores, rather than scaled scores. As a result, student performances often depended on the difficulties of the assessments selected, making it very difficult to achieve objective cross-comparisons. For example, one school doing pull-ups and one doing modified pull-ups could not be compared previously. With scaled scores, the difficulty of an assessment is taken into consideration for the scaling process. Therefore, kindergarten students in first-period class completing the Hopping assessment can be compared to students in second period who completed the Striking assessment

Second, because the difficulty of each item in this set of assessments is known, and the discrimination ability between items is known, teachers can select assessment tasks that target specific levels of student learning. For example, a set of tasks usually is administered to all students; however, very difficult or easy items usually don't work well for students at low or high ends of the ability scale. These students either all score at the top (a Level 4 performance) or at the bottom (Level 1). If that's the case, then the assessment has failed to discriminate and is generally ineffective at providing information about ability. With an assessment bank, assessments with appropriate difficulties for a targeted group can be selected. This selection process, known as computerized adaptive testing, can enable student assessment to be very time-efficient. Teachers can select appropriately difficult assessments for each student, even though the assessments are different.

Third, developing and applying new assessments becomes much easier with an assessment bank. In the past, when existing tests or items became too difficult or too easy for a group of students, separate tests were developed for that group. That meant that scores from the newly developed tests no longer could be interpreted on the basis of the existing tests. The assessment bank concept can solve that problem. Instead of developing new tests, one can develop additional assessments targeted to the population to be tested, then link them to the existing bank. As a result, assessments sharing the same scale are accumulated, and a complete bank can be formed gradually.

Finally, an assessment bank makes accurate assessment of student change/growth possible. Previously, when it became obvious that a task was either too difficult or too easy for a student or groups of students, a different test was developed for them. The problem with that procedure is that the "new" test wasn't related to the original one, and teachers had no way to determine what a student's ability would be on the original test. An assessment bank can eliminate that problem because the scores will be equivalent, even if they're generated from different tasks.

Think of the process in this way: Suppose that you want to determine a student's upper-body strength and use a pull-up test as the assessment. You would see a lot of "0" scores, because the test was too difficult. A push-up assessment, on the other hand, would yield far fewer "0" scores, and the range of scores would be wider. Unless you have established a link between the two assessments, you would have no way to equate a score of one pull-up to a score of five push-ups. The process used in the PE Metrics assessment project allows teachers and researchers to equate different scores across assessments.

Calibration of Standard 1 Assessments
Samples & Data Collection

Using 30 Standard 1 assessments described earlier, more than 4,000 students were assessed at some 90 schools across the country, making this project one of the largest and most comprehensive analyses of the current state of movement performance among elementary school students in physical education. For each class of students, at least two assessments were administered, along with at least one common assessment so that assessments with one grade can be set onto the same scale. In most cases, all assessments were given in the same week or on the same day. In addition, a selected sample was administered linking assessments so that scales across grades can be linked.

Statistical data analyses. Analyses of the national sample included extensive traditional test-construction methodology, such as item difficulty ratings and discrimination indices, which established evidence of validity. A more contemporary analysis using IRT also was applied to establish validity.

This cutting-edge approach examined item difficulty and discrimination for the purpose of equating assessments across grades and within grade levels. Equating allows teachers to compare students of different grades on different assessments. For example, teachers can compare 2nd-graders' jumping with 5th-graders' inline skating to tell whether the program shows progressive learning. Model data fit and categorization statistics were also established to make sure statistically that the data really represent the entire population.

A Summary of the Results

Tables 1-3 (pp. 24-26) summarize descriptive statistics and frequencies of assessments for kindergarten, grade 2 and grade 5, respectively. Tables 4-6 (pp. 27-28) summarize the difficulty of assessments by grade according to the IRT calibrations. Note that:

A. Both kindergarten and grade 5 assessments are set on the scale of grade 2, so that one can compare a scale score from any of those grades directly.

B. Only assessments' difficulties were reported, and more detailed information for model-data fit statistics and corresponding information for each scoring rubric can be found in a special issue of *Measurement in Physical Education and Exercise Science*. (Visit www.aahperd.org/aapar/publications/journals for more information.)

For an informal assessment practice, teachers can select an assessment based on its difficulty. (The larger the value, the more difficult the task; see tables 4-6.) Keep in mind that difficulty logits were compared to grade 2 assessments. All the kindergarten logits are negative because they are easier than grade 2 logits. That is, compared to other assessments, Weight Transfer is a kindergarten assessment with moderate difficulty (–0.56), Catching is the simplest (–1.52) and Dribble With Hand is most difficult (–0.13).

After administering any assessment, teachers can compare the results with the national statistics summarized in Tables 1-3. For example, teachers who administer the kindergarten Dribble With Hand assessment and calculate the class average to be 2.5 on each dimension will see that the class performed slightly better than the national average. If 50 percent of the class scored a 3 on the rubric's form dimension, teachers also will find from the table that, nationally, only 15.7 percent of kindergartners score a 3.

Calibration of Standards 2-6 Assessments

Standards 2-6 assessments are cognitive test items and have been validated using IRT techniques, also. Because the content of Standards 3 and 4 is similar, one bank of test items was developed for the combined standards. Standards 5 and 6 were combined, similarly. In addition, content from Standard 2, which is based on exercise physiology principles, was moved to the Standards 3 and 4 test, because it's related closely to fitness knowledge.

Because NASPE recognizes that teachers will want to use these tests in a variety of ways, this publication offers two options:

1. The book offers printed question items keyed to specific standards and performance descriptors (pp. 131-154). Teachers may use these items, especially for formative assessments.

2. The CD-ROM accompanying this book also contains the test items, and teachers are encouraged to copy them into a Word document from which to administer items to students. Teachers may use entire tests for a standard or may select items across or within particular standards. Teachers from school districts that buy NASPE's PE Metrics Online will have access to different test items, which also are linked to the same standards and performance descriptors. Teachers may select these items for a test, and students may take the test electronically. PE Metrics Online will score the test and will convert students' raw scores to ability scores. In addition, PE Metrics Online users are able to generate reports for students or parents to explain performance on the test.

A Summary of the Results

For Standards 2-6, displays of test averages and difficulty would be meaningless. Teachers are given the option of using an entire test of one standard, of selecting small numbers of questions in one standard, or of selecting small numbers of questions across all standards. In the construction of these test questions, any questions for which more than 90 percent of a national sample answered correctly, or for which more than 90 percent answered incorrectly, were omitted from the test. Therefore, no question was unusually easy or difficult. The overall test difficulty was not computed, as most teachers will not administer the entire test as is.

Conclusion

Based on the analyses conducted, teachers should be confident that PE Metrics assessments provide a clear and meaningful set of attainable expectations for students. The format and descriptive information in the rubrics provide students and teachers with targets for improved performance. The cognitive items provide teachers with a basis for knowledge expected as a result of student learning. In addition, researchers benefit from data analyses that are far more thorough than traditional skills tests analysis. As such, PE Metrics addresses the needs of teachers and students who will be the end users of the assessments, as well as researchers who can use the assessments as an example of new and dynamic measurement.

Table 1: Kindergarten Standard 1 Descriptive Statistics & Frequencies

Assessment	Mean	SD	n	% Students at Each Criterion Level				
				0	1	2	3	4
Dribble With Hand								
Form	2.05	1.16	562	0.2	46.1	20.3	15.7	17.8
Continuous Action & Control	2.11	1.10	562	0.2	39.1	26.2	18.3	16.2
Hopping								
Form	2.36	1.05	478	0.6	28.5	18.0	40.0	13.0
Consistency of Action	2.65	0.93	479	0.6	12.8	24.7	44.8	17.2
Running								
Form	2.86	0.74	264	0.4	0.8	30.3	49.2	19.3
Consistency of Action	2.42	0.78	264	0.4	9.5	45.5	37.1	7.6
Sliding								
Form	2.71	0.81	474	0.8	6.1	27.8	51.9	13.3
Consistency of Action	2.88	0.72	474	0.2	5.5	14.8	65.6	13.9
Striking								
Form	2.55	0.87	313	0.3	15.3	22.4	53.0	8.9
Continuous Strikes & Boundaries	2.20	0.95	313	0.3	29.1	28.4	34.8	7.3
Underhand Catching								
Form	2.81	0.74	202	0	4.0	28.2	48.0	19.8
Catching Success	2.98	0.70	202	0	3.0	18.8	55.0	23.3
Underhand Throw								
Form	2.29	0.67	185	3.2	3.8	54.1	37.3	1.6
Distance & Boundaries	2.28	0.62	185	3.2	4.3	54.6	37.3	0.5
Weight Transfer								
Form	2.22	0.92	150	2.0	18.0	32.7	36.0	11.3
Weight Support & Control	2.95	0.52	150	0.7	0.7	6.7	78.0	14.0

Table 2: Grade 2 Standard 1 Descriptive Statistics & Frequencies

Assessment	Mean	SD	n	% Students at Each Criterion Level				
				0	1	2	3	4
Approach & Kick a Ball								
Form (first trial)	2.38	0.86	120	0.8	13.3	42.5	34.2	9.2
Dance Sequence								
Patterns & Transitions	2.06	0.70	120	1.7	16.7	55.8	25.8	0
Beat of the Music	2.10	0.63	120	0	15.0	60.0	25.0	0
Dribble With Hand & Jog								
Form	2.30	0.77	1142	0.4	14.9	42.0	39.6	3.1
Space & Distance	2.29	0.81	1142	0.4	16.6	40.7	37.7	4.5
Ball Control	2.33	0.75	1142	0.4	13.2	41.2	43.0	2.2
Galloping								
Form	2.22	1.02	234	0.4	26.9	37.6	20.1	15.0
Consistency	2.79	0.94	234	0.4	7.7	30.3	35.0	26.5
Gymnastics Sequence								
Still Beginning and End	2.21	0.76	173	1.7	9.8	59.5	23.7	5.2
Balances	2.21	0.93	173	1.7	19.7	43.9	24.9	9.8
Weight Transfer	2.18	0.80	173	0.6	20.2	42.2	34.7	2.3
Jump Forward								
Form	2.72	0.80	953	0.2	8.0	28.2	41.9	20.9
Distance	2.78	0.64	953	0.2	2.1	31.1	44.2	21.5
Jumping & Landing Combination								
Jump On to the Box	2.20	1.01	148	0.7	29.7	29.7	29.1	10.8
Jump Off of the Box	2.41	0.96	148	0.7	18.9	31.8	35.8	12.8
Locomotor Sequence								
Locomotor Pattern	2.10	0.83	166	0	24.7	45.8	24.7	4.8
Transitions	2.00	0.89	166	0.6	30.1	45.2	16.9	7.2
Overhand Catching								
Form	2.61	0.88	181	1.7	8.8	33.2	41.4	14.9
Catches the ball	2.80	0.81	181	2.2	2.2	28.7	49.2	17.7
Skipping								
Form	3.34	0.89	226	1.3	4.4	6.6	34.1	53.5
Consistency	3.34	0.89	226	1.3	4.4	6.6	34.1	53.5
Striking With Paddle								
Success	2.57	0.74	182	0	10.4	26.4	58.8	4.4
Control	2.02	0.90	118	0	37.4	25.8	34.6	2.2

Table 3: Grade 5 Standard 1 Descriptive Statistics & Frequencies

Assessment	Mean	SD	n	% Students at Each Criterion Level				
				0	1	2	3	4
Basketball Defense								
Defensive Stance	2.53	0.98	169	0	14.8	37.9	26.6	20.7
Blocks Passing Lanes	2.67	0.82	169	0	6.5	35.5	42.0	16.0
Aggressive Defense	2.57	0.81	169	0	5.9	45.0	34.9	14.2
Basketball: Dribble, Pass & Receive								
Dribbling	2.00	0.74	238	0.8	21.8	56.3	18.1	2.9
Passing	2.39	1.14	238	1.3	25.6	28.6	21.4	23.1
Receiving	2.71	1.10	238	0	18.5	23.9	25.6	31.9
Basketball Offense								
Movement Without the Ball	2.65	0.96	232	0	12.1	32.8	33.2	22.0
Passing	2.71	0.82	232	0	6.5	32.8	44.0	16.8
Receiving	3.17	0.78	232	0	2.2	16.8	42.7	38.4
Dance								
Steps	2.48	0.98	94	0	19.1	29.8	35.1	16.0
Sequence	2.63	0.92	94	0	13.8	25.5	44.7	16.0
Beat of the Music	2.61	0.86	94	0	10.6	31.9	43.6	13.8
Floor Hockey: Dribble & Shoot								
Dribble	2.00	1.11	101	1.0	42.6	26.7	14.9	14.9
Shoot	2.33	0.97	101	0	17.8	49.5	14.9	17.8
Gymnastics								
Composition	2.73	1.03	100	0	16.0	22.0	35.0	27.0
Technique	2.96	1.02	100	0	10.0	24.0	26.0	40.0
Transitions	3.43	0.83	100	0	4.2	10.4	25.0	61.0
Inline Skating								
Forward Stride	2.46	1.14	99	1.0	24.2	26.3	24.2	24.2
Changing Direction	1.95	0.86	99	1.0	30.3	47.5	15.2	6.1
Stopping	2.56	0.77	99	1.0	2.0	49.5	35.4	12.1
Soccer: Dribble, Pass & Receive								
Dribbling	1.76	0.74	581	0.2	40.6	44.4	13.0	1.7
Passing	2.10	0.97	581	0	32.2	35.5	22.4	10.0
Receiving	2.31	0.99	581	0	25.0	32.0	29.6	13.4
Soccer Offense								
Movement Without the Ball	2.32	0.98	34	0	23.5	32.4	32.4	11.8
Passing	2.47	0.86	34	0	14.7	32.4	44.1	8.8
Receiving	2.59	0.74	34	0	5.9	38.2	47.1	8.8

Continued on next page

Table 3: Grade 5 Standard 1 Descriptive Statistics & Frequencies *(Cont.)*

Assessment	Mean	SD	n	% Students at Each Criterion Level				
				0	1	2	3	4
Overhand Throwing								
Form	2.66	0.94	172	0	12.2	32.0	33.1	22.7
Accuracy to Target	3.32	0.62	172	0	0.6	9.3	50.0	40.1
Striking With a Paddle								
Form	1.65	0.99	629	1.7	59.6	18.3	12.6	7.8
Continuous Strikes	1.29	0.78	629	2.4	78.7	11.1	2.9	4.9

Table 4: Summary of Calibration for Kindergarten

Assessment Number	Name	n	Difficulty Logit
1	Catching	1182	-1.52
2	Dribble With Hand	1060	-0.13
3	Hopping	914	-0.64
4	Running	514	-0.93
5	Weight Transfer	568	-0.56
6	Underhand Throwing	1092	-0.38
7	Sliding (L)	894	-0.65
8	Striking (L)	616	-0.28

Note: L = Linking tasks administered across grades

Table 5. Summary of Calibration for Grade 2

Assessments Number	Name	n	Difficulty Logit
1	Sliding (L)	148	-0.65
2	Striking (L)	328	-0.28
3	Approach & Kick a Ball	360	0.04
4	Dance Sequence	240	0.01
5	Dribble With Hand & Jog	3399	0.24
6	Gymnastics Sequence	513	0.48
7	Jump Forward	5658	-0.43
8	Locomotor Sequence	326	0.8
9	Overhand Catching	1086	-0.42
10	Skipping	448	-1.31
11	Striking With Paddle	360	0.5
12	Galloping (L)	448	0.11
13	Jumping & Landing Combination (L)	282	0.92

Table 6. Summary of Calibration for Grade 5

Assessments Number	Name	n	Difficulty Logit
1	Galloping (L)	250	0.11
2	Jumping & Landing Combination (L)	284	0.92
3	Basketball: Dribble, Pass & Receive	711	-0.51
4	Basketball: Defense	498	-0.51
5	Basketball: Offense	672	-1.26
6	Dance	282	-0.57
7	Floor Hockey	202	0.1
8	Gymnastics	300	-1.06
9	Inline Skating	291	-1.07
10	Soccer: Dribble, Pass & Receive	1731	-0.2
11	Soccer: Offense	102	-1.18
12	Overhand Throwing	1020	-1.03
13	Striking With a Paddle	1258	0.44

Frequently Asked Questions About PE Metrics

Over the years of developing PE Metrics, teachers have asked many questions at conference presentations and during conversations. In this chapter, we have summarized the most frequently asked questions, and present our responses.

Q: PE Metrics recommends video-recording the assessments for Standard 1. Why should I video-record the assessments?

A: We recommend video-recording in general because we have seen teachers' surprise when seeing a student's performance on screen. Problems in performance are easy to miss when you're involved in teaching. Video-recording allows you to go back and review a student's performance. Also, if you're assessing for summative assessment, you will find it helpful to have a video record of student performance, because you then will have solid evidence documenting student achievement.

Q: I don't have the time to video my classes and then view the recordings. Can I just score students live as they complete the assessments in class?

A: You can do that for some assessments. If the skill is fairly simple (e.g., hopping, skipping, or striking with a paddle), you can score "live" on the score sheet or personal digital assistant. We recommend recording more complex assessments (e.g., grade 5 soccer offense or basketball defense), so that you can view each student individually and more than once, if necessary. The more you do that, the easier it gets and the more efficient you become. You also will find that you will be a better observer in your teaching.

Q: What are the protocols used in Standard 1 and why are they important?

A: The protocols in each assessment provide information on exactly how to administer the assessments. Following the protocols exactly as written provides valid and reliable skills assessment and allows for comparisons to students across the country.

Q: I don't have the exact equipment — such as an 8-inch playground ball — or space that the assessments call for. Can I substitute a soccer ball or reduce the size of the space?

A: Yes, you can, if you're using the assessment for your own students only. You can adjust the equipment, space or trials to meet your needs, so long as you make the same changes for all students. If, however, you change the assessment again in the following semester or year, you can't compare your own classes over time or your classes with someone else's classes. You must be consistent if you want to compare student scores over time.

Note that substituting equipment or space alters the assessment significantly. The assessment won't be the same without following the protocols and equipment requirements exactly as written. While physical education teachers are used to "making do," if you change any aspect of the assessments in PE Metrics, you can't compare your students' scores to the national scores or upload scores into the national database.

Q: How can I supervise my class, operate the video camera and ensure meaningful participation in my large classes and still conduct Standard 1 assessments?

A: It's challenging to maintain control of the class and ensure that all students are participating safely in an activity when conducting the assessments. Here are some suggestions:

- Assess in groups, if possible. Many of the assessments suggest having more than one student perform at one time. If you're video-recording for later viewing, students might be able to perform in larger groups.
- Use a number of stations related to the class objective in which students work in small groups rotating from station to station, one of which can be the assessment station. For example, you can assess students at one station, making sure that you can see the entire teaching space while you're assessing. Other groups of students could be peer-assessing, practicing the actual assessment or self-assessing. Or, they could be working on other skills related to your current or past activities. You need to have taught students how to work in groups at stations and have clear directions for the task at each station.
- You don't need to assess all you students the same day; take 10 minutes out of each class and assess a handful of students.
- If you have a college intern or observer, use him or her for supervision or video-recording.
- With the younger elementary grades, the classroom teacher might be willing to stay for the class to help out.

Q: I have my students only twice a week. How can I use PE Metrics assessments without taking up half of my teaching time?

A: Here are some suggestions:

- You don't need to assess everyone on the same day. Take 10 or 15 minutes out of a class and assess a handful of students. The assessments can be completed over several days.
- Ask for help from aides, parent volunteers or older students.
- Assess in groups, if possible, to save time.
- If the assessment is fairly simple (e.g., hopping, skipping), you might be able to assess part or all of the students while the entire class is participating in the activity.

The use of assessments represents a learning opportunity for students, not lost teaching time. Instruction that includes assessment provides important feedback to students regarding achievement. In other words, assessment should be part of instruction, and students should be learning how well they're meeting the criteria when participating in the assessment.

Q: It's so overwhelming to think about all this assessment. How can I get started?

A: Begin with small, manageable steps, such as starting your assessments with a favorite unit. You can learn how to administer an assessment with those skills that you're very confident teaching and evaluating, and introduce procedures and responsibilities to the students gradually. If problems arise, you can make changes for the next time.

You also can conduct PE Metrics assessments for a few activities in each grade level per year. For example, you might wish to assess all kindergarteners to see how well they meet the criteria in the locomotor skills (e.g., hopping, sliding, throwing) that you've focused on.

Try conducting a sequence of assessments of similar tasks from K to grade 5. For example, begin with a single isolated skill, such as the Kindergarten Dribble with Hand (stationary), and progress to skill combinations such as Grade 2 Dribble with Hand and Jog, and Grade 5 Dribble, Pass and Receive a Ball with a Partner.

Q: I don't teach many of the activities in the PE Metrics assessments. How can they help me?

A: PE Metrics is designed to reflect a consensus of critical outcomes and provide examples of assessments. We encourage you to use the assessments in PE Metrics as a foundation to develop your own assessments that align with your teaching objectives. Examples include:

- Consider the Standard 1 rubrics to be templates. For example, you could modify the soccer rubric to assess floor hockey or any other invasion game, because many of the essential criteria are similar.
- Share or develop new assessments with colleagues before assessing students. More perspectives will help you avoid ineffective assessments and save revision time later.
- Practice and score the assessment with a few students.
- Give and score the assessment with one class of students before using the data to make instruction or grading decisions.
- Each criterion in the Standard 1 assessments should include only essential elements. Including too many elements in one criterion makes understanding and scoring difficult.
- Choose a limited number of Standards 2–6 questions that might fit your curriculum and then use them as examples to develop your own questions.

Q: How am I to use the online videos?

A: The videos found by visiting www.pemetrics.org were designed to help you use the observation rubrics accurately. They provide a video example of competent performance and common errors for each of the Standard 1 assessments. Before you score students on an assessment, access the video for that assessment and review the expectations for performing each level of the rubric.

Q: What if I want to assess my students at levels other than kindergarten or grades 2 or 5?

A: The assessments in PE Metrics are designed as exit criteria for each standard at the designated grade level: K, 2 or 5. However, you can use any of the assessments for other grade levels, as appropriate. For example, if your kindergarten students have physical education only one time per week, they may not achieve competence in the kindergarten assessments until 1st grade.

Also, if you have a grade 5 student with special needs, but he or she demonstrates the gross motor or cognitive development of a younger child, it might be more appropriate to assess that student using a grade 2 assessment.

Conversely, if some 3rd-grade students have achieved Level 3 competence earlier than the designated grade-level assessment, you might challenge them by introducing them to the higher level skills identified in the grade 5 assessments.

Q: I have collected a lot of assessment scores from my students. What can I do with the data?

A: Here are some suggestions:

- Use the scores to demonstrate student improvement over time.
- Use the evidence of student learning to advocate for your program at the school and school district levels.
- Provide summary reports for parents on their children's progress.
- Use the scores to identify strengths and weakness in your program and then, to plan your curriculum.
- Provide feedback to students on their level of performance.
- Write a brief article on your students' accomplishments for a school or district newsletter.
- Use the assessment data as feedback on your teaching. Are the students learning what you think you're teaching them?

Q: In regard to the Standards 2–6 tests, what if I don't teach everything in the test bank?

A: You should choose those questions from the bank that fit your curriculum. In other words, if you teach fitness concepts at all grade levels, choose questions that assess those concepts specifically. You also could modify your curriculum to address more concepts in Standards 2–6.

Q: What is the national database and why should I consider contributing to it?

A: NASPE is in the process of creating PE Metrics Online, a Web site that will allow teachers who administer the tests using the correct protocols to add their scores to the national database. If you choose to upload your students' scores, they will be added to all the other national data. In that way, PE Metrics can be updated with scores from across the country, and you can contribute to our profession's leading efforts in assessment.

Standard 1 Assessments

Kindergarten Assessments
Dribble With Hand
Hopping
Running
Sliding
Striking
Underhand Catching
Underhand Throw
Weight Transfer

Grade 2 Assessments
Approach & Kick a Ball
Dance Sequence
Dribble With Hand & Jog
Galloping
Gymnastics Sequence
Jump Forward
Jumping & Landing Combination
Locomotor Sequence
Overhand Catching
Skipping
Striking With a Paddle

Grade 5 Assessments
Basketball: Defense
Basketball: Dribble, Pass & Receive
Basketball: Offense
Dance
Floor Hockey: Dribble & Shoot
Gymnastics
Inline Skating
Overhand Throwing
Soccer: Dribble, Pass & Receive
Soccer: Offense
Striking With a Paddle

Standard 1:

Demonstrates competency in motor skills and movement patterns needed to perform a variety of physical activities.

Performance Indicator:

Throw, catch, dribble, kick and strike from a stationary position.

Assessment Task:

Dribble a ball continuously for 15 seconds with one hand.

Criteria for Competence (Level 3):

1. Dribbles with all the selected essential elements:

   a) one-hand contact.

   b) maintains constant height of rebound.

   c) pushes ball (no slapping).

2. Maintains a continuous dribble with feet staying within boundaries.

■ Assessment Rubric:

Level	1. Form	2. Continuous Action & Control
4	Dribbles with all the selected essential elements with fluid motion.	Maintains a continuous dribble for 15 seconds with very little travel from the starting position.
3	Dribbles with all the selected essential elements: a) one-hand contact. b) maintains constant height of rebound. c) pushes ball (no slapping).	Maintains a continuous dribble with feet staying within boundaries.
2	Dribbles with 2 of 3 essential elements present.	1 break in continuous dribble or moves outside of boundaries on one occasion.
1	Dribbles with 1 or no essential elements present.	Has more than 1 break in continuous dribble and/or moves outside of boundaries on more than one occasion.
0	Violates safety procedures and/or does not complete the assessment task.	

■ **Assessment Protocols:**

Directions for Students (Read aloud, verbatim):
- Today, I am going to watch you dribble.
- On my signal, start dribbling the ball using one hand, keeping the ball bouncing at the same height, pushing the ball without slapping it.
- Stay in your own square.
- Continue dribbling until I give the stop signal.

Directions for Teachers:

Preparation:
- See the chapter titled Procedures to Administer & Score PE Metrics Assessments for instruction, warm-up, camera location and operation.
- Three students can be assessed at one time.
- Clearly indicate each student's personal space (3-foot square).
- Use your own start/stop signal allowing students to dribble for 15 seconds.
- The assessment is 1 trial (15 seconds).

Safety:
- Be sure that students understand where their own square is located.
- If outside, use smooth, hard surface that is free of obstructions.

Equipment/Materials:
- 3 properly inflated 10" playground balls.
- Taped 3-foot squares on floor to designate personal space.
- Stopwatch or clock for timing 15 seconds.

Diagram of Space/Distances:

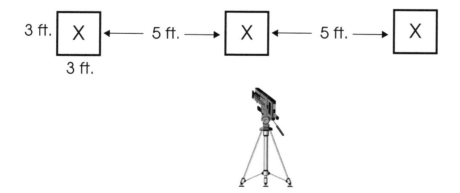

Camera Location and Operation:

Set up camera in front of the middle student and far enough away so that all 3 students can be viewed. The students' entire bodies, including the feet, must be in view and close enough to assess the form.

Assessment Score Sheet

PE Teacher _____   Grade _____   Date _____

School _____   Classroom Teacher _____

Student Name	ID Number	Gender	Form (0-4)	Continuous Action & Control (0-4)	Total Score (0-8) 6=Competent

K Grade
Hopping

Standard 1:

Demonstrates competency in motor skills and movement patterns needed to perform a variety of physical activities.

Performance Indicator:

Demonstrate hopping, jumping, galloping and sliding.

Assessment Task:

Hop in place.

Criteria for Competence (Level 3):

1. Hops, taking off from one foot and landing on the same foot. Performs action on other foot
2. Hops within self-space continuously for 10 seconds with no loss of balance or extraneous arm motion. Performs action on other foot

■ Assessment Rubric:

Level	1. Form*	2. Consistency of Action
4	Hops, taking off from one foot and landing on the same foot with smooth, balanced action. Performs action correctly on other foot.	Hops within self-space continuously for 10 seconds, with fluid motion and consistency on each foot.
3	Hops, taking off from one foot and landing on the same foot. Performs action on other foot.	Hops within self-space continuously for 10 seconds, with no loss of balance or extraneous arm motion. Performs action on other foot.
2	Performs hopping action correctly for one but not the other foot.	Hops continuously for 10 seconds, with no loss of balance, but does not stay in self-space.
1	Performs hopping action incorrectly for both feet.	Loses balance or cannot sustain hopping motion on both left and right feet for 10 seconds.
0	Violates safety procedures and/or does not complete the assessment task.	

*Example of incorrect hopping action includes: foot does not leave the floor, one foot to the other foot, and one foot to two feet.

■ **Assessment Protocols:**

Directions for Students (Read aloud, verbatim):

- Today, I am going to watch you hop.
- Stand in the middle of your own square.
- On my signal, start hopping on one foot in your square until I give the stop signal.
- Then, I will ask you to switch to your other foot.
- I am looking to see if you take off and land on the same foot without stopping or moving outside your square for 10 seconds.

Directions for Teachers:

Preparation:

- See the chapter titled Procedures to Administer & Score PE Metrics Assessments for instruction, warm-up, camera location and operation.
- Three students can be assessed at one time.
- Clearly indicate each student's personal square (3-foot square).
- Use your own start/stop signal allowing students to hop for 10 seconds on each foot.

Safety:

- Be sure that students understand where their personal space is located.
- Allow only safe footwear (no sandals, boots, bare feet, etc.).
- If outside, use smooth, hard surface that is free of obstructions.

Equipment/Materials:

- Taped 3-foot squares to designate personal-space area.
- Stopwatch or clock for timing 10 seconds.

Diagram of Space/Distances:

Use taped 3-foot squares on the floor to designate personal-space area for 3 students, with 5 feet between each.

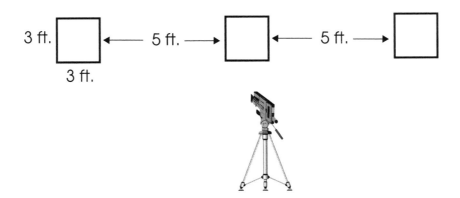

Camera Location and Operation:

Set up camera in front of the middle student and far enough away so that all 3 students can be viewed. The students' entire bodies, including the feet, must be in view and close enough to assess the form.

Assessment Score Sheet

PE Teacher _____   Grade _____   Date _____

School _____   Classroom Teacher _____

Student Name	ID Number	Gender	Form (0-4)	Consistency of Action (0-4)	Total Score (0-8) 6=Competent

Standard 1:

Demonstrates competency in motor skills and movement patterns needed to perform a variety of physical activities.

Performance Indicator:

Demonstrate a mature pattern of running.

Assessment Task:

Run continuously for 60 feet.

Criteria for Competence (Level 3):

1. Runs with the essential elements of a mature pattern:

   a) arm/leg opposition.

   b) toes point forward.

   c) arms swing forward/backward and do not cross midline of body.

   d) feet land heel to toe.

2. Runs in straight pathway without stumbling, stopping or falling down.

■ Assessment Rubric:

Level	1. Form	2. Consistency of Action
4	Displays all the essential elements of a mature pattern, with fluid motion.	Runs smoothly in straight pathway, without breaks in stride.
3	Runs with the essential elements of a mature pattern: a) arm /leg opposition. b) toes point forward. c) arms swing forward/backward and do not cross midline of body. d) feet land heel to toe.	Runs in straight pathway without stumbling, stopping or falling down.
2	Runs with 3 of 4 essential elements present.	Runs without stopping or falling down, but stumbles, runs in erratic pathway or has inconsistent stride.
1	Runs with 2 or fewer essential elements present.	Stops running action or falls down.
0	Violates safety procedures and/or does not complete the assessment task.	

■ **Assessment Protocols:**

Directions for Students (Read aloud, verbatim):

- Today, I am going to watch you run.
- Stand behind the starting line.
- On my signal, run fast all the way through the course.
- Stay in the running lane by running in a straight line.
- Do not stop running until after you cross the finish line.
- Run as fast as you can, showing me your best running form by swinging your arms forward and backward, having your toes pointed forward and landing on the heel of your foot first.

Directions for Teachers:

Preparation:

- See the chapter titled Procedures to Administer & Score PE Metrics Assessments for instruction, warm-up, camera location and operation.
- The assessment can be set up inside or outside.
- Clearly indicate the running lane area and finish line.
- Emphasize to students that they should not stop running until **after** they cross the finish line.

Safety:

- Be sure that students understand where the finish line is located.
- Allow only safe footwear (no sandals, boots, bare feet, etc.).
- If outside, use smooth, safe surface that is free of obstructions.

Equipment/Materials:

- 4 cones to mark the starting line and finish line.

Diagram of Space/Distances:

Use cones to form a lane 5 feet wide and 60 feet long, with an additional 15 feet of unobstructed space beyond the finish line (total of 75 feet long). Starting line is at least 3 feet from any obstruction, and finish line is at least 15 feet from any obstruction.

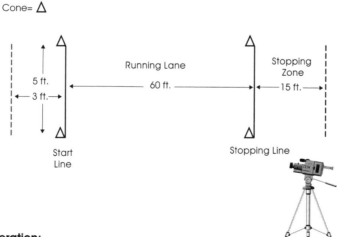

Camera Location and Operation:

Set up camera near end of running lane but outside cones, so that student can be viewed running toward the finish line. The student's entire body, including the feet, must be in view and close enough to assess the form. Be sure that you can view student's form from start to finish.

Assessment Score Sheet

PE Teacher _____ Grade _____ Date _____

School _____ Classroom Teacher _____

Student Name	ID Number	Gender	Form (0-4)	Consistency of Action (0-4)	Total Score (0-8) 6=Competent

K Grade
Sliding

Standard 1:

Demonstrates competency in motor skills and movement patterns needed to perform a variety of physical activities.

Performance Indicator:

Demonstrate hopping, jumping, galloping and sliding.

Assessment Task:

Slide continuously for 30 feet, with the preferred foot leading.

Criteria for Competence (Level 3):

1. Slides with selected essential elements:
   a) uses a step-close action.
   b) maintains a side orientation without twisting hips (lead foot may turn out slightly in the direction of the slide).
   c) same foot leading.
   d) brief period of non-support.
2. Slides without losing continuity of the action.

■ Assessment Rubric:

Level	1. Form	2. Consistency of Action
4	Displays all the selected essential elements, with fluid motion.	Slides smoothly without losing continuity of the action.
3	Slides with selected essential elements: a) uses a step-close action. b) maintains a side orientation without twisting hips (lead foot may turn out slightly). c) same foot leading. d) brief period of non-support.	Slides without losing continuity of the action.
2	Slides with 3 of 4 essential elements.	Loses the continuity of the action.
1	Slides with 2 or fewer essential elements.	Stops sliding action or falls down.
0	Violates safety procedures and/or does not complete the assessment task.	

■ **Assessment Protocols:**

Directions for Students (Read aloud, verbatim):

- Today, I am going to watch you slide.
- Stand with your side to the starting line.
- On my signal, slide to the end of the lane, without stopping, and cross the finish line.
- Stay in the lane.
- This is not a race.
- Show me your best sliding form by:

    a) using a step/close pattern with the same foot leading;

    b) moving sideways without twisting your hips.

Directions for Teachers:

Preparation:

- See the chapter titled Procedures to Administer & Score PE Metrics Assessments for instruction, warm-up, camera location and operation.
- Clearly indicate the lane area, and start and finish lines.

Safety:

- Be sure that students understand where the end lines are located.
- Allow only safe footwear (no sandals, boots, bare feet, etc.).
- If outside, use a smooth, hard surface that is free of obstructions.

Equipment/Materials:

- 4 cones and floor tape to mark the starting line and finish line.

Diagram of Space/Distances:

Use cones to form a lane 5 feet wide and 30 feet long, with an additional 15 feet of unobstructed space beyond the finish line (total of 45 feet long). Starting line is at least 3 feet from any obstruction, and finish line at least 15 feet from any obstruction.

Cone= △

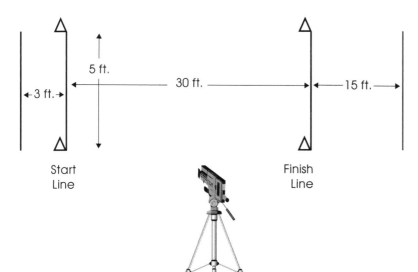

Start
Line

Finish
Line

Camera Location and Operation:

Set up camera at middle of lane outside cones so that student (and the start and finish lines) can be viewed for the entire sliding motion while facing the camera. The student's entire body, including the feet, must be in view and close enough to assess the form without moving the camera to follow the action.

Assessment Score Sheet

PE Teacher _____ Grade _____ Date _____

School _____ Classroom Teacher _____

Student Name	ID Number	Gender	Form (0-4)	Consistency of Action (0-4)	Total Score (0-8) 6=Competent

Standard 1:

Demonstrates competency in motor skills and movement patterns needed to perform a variety of physical activities.

Performance Indicator:

Throw, catch, dribble, kick and strike from a stationary position.

Assessment Task:

Strike a balloon continuously with a short-handled paddle for 20 seconds using an underhand pattern.

Criteria for Competence (Level 3):

1. Displays all selected essential elements, with no more than 2 errors in form during the entire assessment:
   a) visual tracking.
   b) flat paddle surface.
   c) upward underhand striking pattern using one hand.
2. Displays all of essential elements:
   a) consistently sends the balloon higher than the head.
   b) stays within the boundaries.
   c) maintains continuous striking action.

■ Assessment Rubric:

Level	1. Form	2. Continuous Strikes & Boundaries
4	Displays all selected essential elements with fluid motion and without error.	Always sends the balloon higher than the head. Maintains continous striking action. Very little travel from the starting position.
3	Displays all selected essential elements, with no more that 2 errors in form during the entire assessment: a) visual tracking. b) flat paddle surface. c) upward underhand striking pattern using one hand.	Displays all of essential elements: a) consistently sends the balloon higher than the head. b) stays within the boundaries. c) maintains continuous striking action.
2	Displays all the selected essential elements, with no more than 3 errors in form during the entire assessment.	Strikes with 2 of the 3 essential elements present.
1	Displays all the selected essential elements, with 4 or more errors in form during the entire assessment.	Strikes with 1 or no essential elements present.
0	Violates safety procedures and/or does not complete the assessment task.	

Consistently = 90% and above   Usually = 75% - 89%   Sometimes = 50% -74%   Seldom = below 50%

■ Assessment Protocols:

Directions for Students (Read aloud, verbatim):

- Today, I am going to watch you strike a balloon with a paddle.
- I am looking to see if you keep the paddle flat, watch the balloon and use a one-handed underhand motion.
- Strike the balloon at your waist, but make it go higher than your head.
- Keep the balloon in the air.
- You should stay within your personal square. If you go outside your space, continue striking and try to move back into the square.
- Keep striking the balloon until I say stop. If the balloon falls to the floor, pick it up and resume.

Directions for Teachers:

Preparation:

- See the chapter titled Procedures to Administer & Score PE Metrics Assessments for instruction, warm-up, camera location and operation.
- Clearly indicate the personal-space area.
- The assessment is 20 seconds.

Safety:

- Be sure that students understand where their personal space is located.
- If outside, use a smooth, hard surface that is free of obstructions.

Equipment/Materials:

- 1 short-handled foam, wooden or plastic paddle.
- 1 balloon per student (round balloons inflated fully).
- Floor tape.
- Stopwatch or clock for timing.

Diagram of Space/Distances:

Create a 10-ft.-by-10-ft. square with floor tape to designate personal-space area.

S = Student

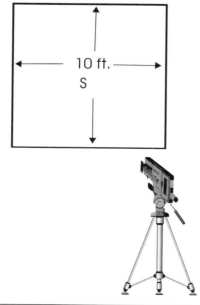

Camera Location and Operation:

Set up camera in front of the student and far enough away so that the entire personal-space area can be viewed. The student's entire body, including the feet, must be in view and close enough to assess the form.

Assessment Score Sheet

PE Teacher _____   Grade _____   Date _____

School _____   Classroom Teacher _____

Student Name	ID Number	Gender	Form (0-4)	Continuous Strikes & Boundaries (0-4)	Total Score (0-8) 6=Competent

K Grade
Underhand Catching

Standard 1:

Demonstrates competency in motor skills and movement patterns needed to perform a variety of physical activities.

Performance Indicator:

Throw, catch, dribble, kick and strike from a stationary position.

Assessment Task:

Catch a ball tossed by a teacher, using an underhand catching pattern.

Criteria for Competence: (Level 3)

1. Attempts the catch with selected essential elements:

   a) hands reach to meet the ball.

   b) uses hands without trapping ball against chest.

   c) does not turn head away from ball.

2. Catches the ball successfully.

■ Assessment Rubric:

Level	1. Form	2. Catching Success
4	Displays all the selected essential elements, with fluid motion.	Catches the ball, with no bobbles.
3	Attempts the catch with selected essential elements: a) hands reach to meet ball. b) uses hands without trapping ball against chest. c) does not turn head away from ball.	Catches the ball successfully.
2	Attempts to catch, with 2 of 3 essential elements present.	Catches the ball, then fumbles and recovers it.
1	Attempts to catch, with 1 or no essential elements.	Catches the ball, then drops it or fails to catch it.
0	Violates safety procedures and/or does not complete the assessment task.	

■ **Assessment Protocols:**

Directions for Students (Read aloud, verbatim):

- Today, I am going to watch you catch.
- Get ready to catch the ball that I am throwing underhand to you.
- You don't have to stay on the starting spot. You may move to catch the ball.
- Show me your best catching form: hands ready, reach for the ball and catch the ball with your hands.
- You will get 3 chances to catch the ball.

Directions for Teachers:

- See the chapter titled Procedures to Administer & Score PE Metrics Assessments for instruction, warm-up, camera location and operation.
- Clearly indicate where student should stand (6' from teacher).
- Toss ball gently, using underhand action so that ball drops toward student's waist.
- If it is a poor toss, you may repeat the toss. Please indicate verbally on the tape that the toss will be repeated.
  Note: Ball may touch chest after it has been stopped and controlled with the hands.
- Remind students that they may move from the starting spot to catch the ball.
- Score each trial separately.

Safety:

Set up catching area so that no other students can enter it.

Equipment/Materials:

- 1- 8" playground ball.
- 2 spots or lines marked on floor.

Diagram of Space/Distance:

S = Student
T = Teacher

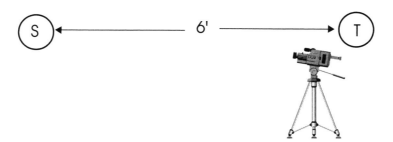

Camera Location and Operation:

Set up camera so that it points directly toward the student. The student's entire body, including the feet, must be in view and close enough to assess the form.

Assessment Score Sheet

PE Teacher _____   Grade _____   Date _____

School _____   Classroom Teacher _____

Student Name	ID Number	Gender	Form- 3 Trials (0-4)			Catching Success 3 Trials (0-4)			Total Score (0-24) 18=Competent
			1st	2nd	3rd	1st	2nd	3rd	

Grade
Underhand Throw K

Standard 1:

Demonstrates competency in motor skills and movement patterns needed to perform a variety of physical activities.

Performance Indicator:

Throw, catch, dribble, kick and strike from a stationary position.

Assessment Task:

Use an underhand throwing pattern to send a ball forward through the air to a large target.

Criteria for Competence (Level 3):

1. Throws with selected essential elements:
   a) arm back in preparation.
   b) opposite foot forward.
   c) releases ball in forward direction.
2. Hits target area on wall.

■ Assessment Rubric:

Level	1. Form	2. Distance & Boundaries
4	Displays all the selected essential elements, with fluid motion.	Hits target area on wall with force.
3	Throws with selected essential elements: a) arm back in preparation. b) opposite foot forward. c) releases ball in forward direction.	Hits target area on wall.
2	Throws with 2 of 3 essential elements present.	Ball airborne for at least 10 feet but does not hit target.
1	Throws with only 1 essential element present.	Ball is airborne less than 10 feet.
0	Violates safety procedures and/or does not complete the assessment task.	

Note: Failure to use underhand throwing pattern (e.g., sidearm or overhand) is Incomplete Assessment Task (0).

■ **Assessment Protocols:**

Directions for Students (Read aloud, verbatim):

- Today, I am going to watch you throw underhand.
- Stand behind the throwing line.
- Do not put your fingers in the holes in the ball.
- On my signal, throw the ball underhand and try to hit the large square on the wall.
- Show me your best throwing form by putting your arm back, stepping with the foot that's on the other side of the arm you are throwing with, and letting go of the ball in a forward direction.
- You will have 3 attempts.

Directions for Teachers:

Preparation:

- See the chapter titled Procedures to Administer & Score PE Metrics Assessments for instruction, warm-up, camera location and operation.
- Clearly indicate the throwing lane on the floor.
- The assessment is 3 attempts.
- Be sure that students do not put their fingers in the whiffle ball holes.
- If assessment is taking place outdoors, it should not be on a windy day.

Safety:

- Set up throwing area so that no other students can enter it.

Equipment/Materials:

- 4 whiffle balls (softball-size) .
- Tape to form throwing line (6-foot line, and target square).
- 4 cones to form throwing lane and the airborne line.

Diagram of Space/Distances:

Use tape to mark a throwing line on the floor 15 feet from a wall. Place another line on the floor 10 feet from the throwing line to mark minimal airborne distance. Mark a 10-foot-by-10-foot target square on the wall. Place the target square 3 feet off the floor. Place a cone at each end of each line.

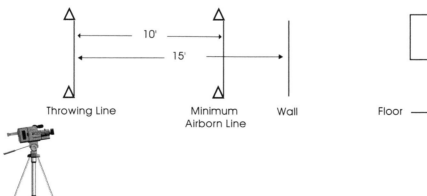

Throwing Line   Minimum   Wall   Floor
                  Airborn Line

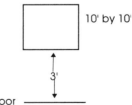

Camera Location and Operation:

Set up camera on an angle so that the student and the wall are visible. The student's entire body, including the feet, must be in view and close enough to assess the form.

Assessment Score Sheet

PE Teacher _____ Grade _____ Date _____

School _____ Classroom Teacher _____

Student Name	ID Number	Gender	Form (0-4) Trials			Distance & Boundaries (0-4) Trials			Total Score (0-24) 18=Competent
			1st	2nd	3rd	1st	2nd	3rd	

K Grade
Weight Transfer

Standard 1:

Demonstrates competency in motor skills and movement patterns needed to perform a variety of physical activities.

Performance Indicator:

Transfer weight hands/feet.

Assessment Task:

Place weight on the hands and transfer feet sideways over a raised bar and back to the starting position.

Criteria for Competence (Level 3):

1. Transfers weight to hands, with selected essential elements:

   a) taking off on 2 feet simultaneously.

   b) landing on 2 feet simultaneously.

   c) hands maintaining stationary contact with the floor.

2. Transfers weight momentarily to hands only, without contacting the bar or without falling down.

■ Assessment Rubric:

Level	1. Form	2. Weight Support & Control
4	Displays all the selected essential elements, with fluid motion.	Transfers weight from feet to hands to feet, with smooth action.
3	Transfers weight to hands, with selected essential elements: a) taking off on 2 feet simultaneously. b) landing on 2 feet simultaneously. c) hands maintaining stationary contact with the floor.	Transfers weight to hands, without feet contacting the bar or without falling down.
2	Transfers weight, with 2 of 3 essential elements present.	Transfers weight to hands without falling down, but feet contact the bar.
1	Transfers weight, with only 1 essential element present.	Feet fail to cross bar, or student falls down.
0	Violates safety procedures and/or does not complete the assessment task.	

■ **Assessment Protocols:**

Directions for Students (Read aloud verbatim):

- Today, I am going to watch you put your weight on your hands.
- Stand on your personal-space marker.
- On my signal, place both hands on the floor, <u>one hand on each side of the line</u>, keeping your feet on the marker.
- On my signal, "Over," take off from two feet, shifting all of your weight onto your hands; cross the bar, without your feet touching it; and land on the other side with two feet.
- Your hands should stay on the floor.
- Then jump your feet back over the line to your marker — two feet taking off, two feet landing at the same time, — then stand up.
- You will do this two times.
- Ready? Over, back, STAND. Wait.
- Ready? Over, back STAND.

Directions for Teachers:

Preparation:

- See the chapter titled Procedures to Administer & Score PE Metrics Assessments for instruction, warm-up, camera location and operation.
- Place a line 6 feet long on the floor. On the back half of the line, place a raised bar 3 feet long and 6 inches high. You might use a yardstick supported by two 6-inch cones. Mark where hands and feet should be placed in starting position. (See diagram.)
- Make 3 stations 5 feet apart. Three students can be assessed at one time.
- Clearly indicate each student's personal marker, where feet should be positioned to begin.
- Have students stand on their markers beside the bar so that all are facing the same direction.
- Be sure to use the commands, "over, back, STAND" for each trial.
- The assessment consists of 2 attempts.

Safety:

- Tape bar to supports (e.g., cones) so that it does not fall off if students hit the bar with their feet.
- If outside, use smooth surface that is free of obstructions.

Equipment/Materials:

- Tape for indicating hand and foot markers, lines and holding bar in place.
- 3 yardsticks (bars).
- 6 6-inch cones.

Diagram of Space/Distances:

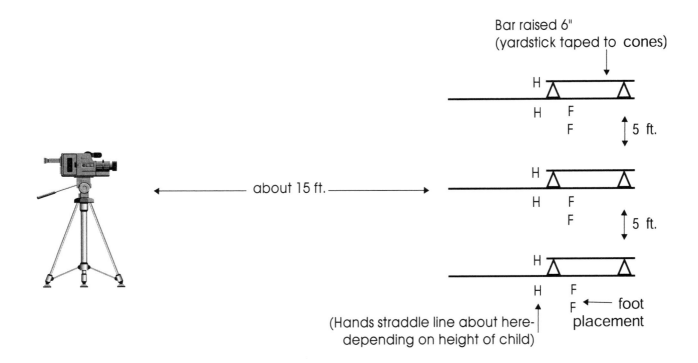

Bar raised 6"
(yardstick taped to cones)

H
H   F
      F   ↕ 5 ft.

H
H   F
      F   ↕ 5 ft.

H
H   F
      F ←— foot
(Hands straddle line about here-   placement
depending on height of child)

←———— about 15 ft. ————→

Camera Location and Operation:

Set up camera in front of the middle student and far enough away so that all 3 students can be viewed. The students' entire bodies, including the feet, must be in view and close enough to assess the form.

Assessment Score Sheet

PE Teacher _____ Grade _____ Date _____

School _____ Classroom Teacher _____

Student Name	ID Number	Gender	Form (0-4) Trials		Wt. Support & Control (0-4) Trials		Total Score (0-16) 12=Competent
			1st	2nd	1st	2nd	

Standard 1:

Demonstrates competency in motor skills and movement patterns needed to perform a variety of physical activities.

Performance Indicator:

Dribble, kick, throw, catch and strike a ball.

Assessment Task:

Approach a stationary ball at a jog and kick with enough force to send it a distance of 30 feet on a smooth, level surface.

Criteria for Competence (Level 3):

1. Kicks from a jog with selected essential elements:

   a) support foot to the side of the ball.

   b) continuous motion into kick.

   c) contact with instep (top of foot/shoelaces).

   d) follow through.

2. Ball reaches target line between the cones.

■ Assessment Rubric:

Level	1. Form	2. Distance & Accuracy
4	Displays all the selected essential elements, with fluid motion.	Ball reaches target line between the cones with good speed.
3	Kicks from a jog, with selected essential elements: a) support foot to the side of the ball. b) continuous motion into kick. c) contact with instep (top of foot/shoelaces). d) follow through.	Ball reaches target line between the cones.
2	Kicks from a jog, with 3 of 4 essential elements present.	Ball doesn't reach target line **or** is not between the cones.
1	Kicks without jogging approach and 2 or fewer essential elements present.	Ball does not reach the target line **and** is not between the cones.
0	Violates safety procedures and/or does not complete the assessment task.	

■ **Assessment Protocols:**

Directions for Students (Read aloud, verbatim):

- Today, I'm going to look at how you kick the ball from a jog.
- On my signal, jog to the ball and kick it, without stopping. Kick it between the cones to the target line.
- Be sure to place your non-kicking foot to the side of the ball, prepare the kicking leg, contact the ball with the top of your foot or shoelaces, and follow through.
- You will kick 3 times.

Directions for Teachers:

Preparation:

- See the chapter titled Procedures to Administer & Score PE Metrics Assessments for instruction, warm-up, camera location and operation.
- Clearly indicate the kicking lane on the floor.
- If assessment is conducted outside, use a hard surface, not grass.
- If keeping the ball stationary is a problem, place a small item under the ball (e.g., gauze, facial cleansing pad, or putty).

Safety:

- Set up kicking area so that no other students can enter it.

Equipment/Materials:

- 4 playground balls (12").
- Tape to form kicking line and target line on floor.
- 8 cones to form kicking lane.

Diagram of Space/Distances:

Use tape to form a kicking line and a target line (30 feet away) on the floor. Each line should be 8 feet long. Kicking line should be at least 10 feet from any obstruction (approach area). Place 4 cones 10 feet apart on each side of the kicking lane, which is 8 feet wide.

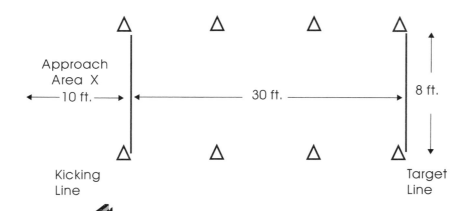

Camera Location and Operation:

Set up camera so that student's aproach, kicking lane and target line can be viewed. The student's entire body, including the feet, must be in view and close enough to assess the form.

Assessment Score Sheet

PE Teacher _____   Grade _____   Date _____

School _____   Classroom Teacher _____

Student Name	ID Number	Gender	Form (0-4)			Distance & Accuracy (0-4)			Total Score (0-24) 18=Competent
			1st	2nd	3rd	1st	2nd	3rd	

2 Grade
Dance Sequence

Standard 1:

Demonstrates competency in motor skills and movement patterns needed to perform a variety of physical activities.

Performance Indicator:

Perform dance sequences to music.

Assessment Task:

Perform to music a grade-level-appropriate individual or partner dance that uses 3 different patterns.

Criteria for Competency (Level 3):

1. Usually performs patterns and transitions correctly.
2. Usually moves to the beat of the music.

■ Assessment Rubric:

Level	1. Patterns & Transitions	2. Beat of the Music
4	Consistently performs patterns and transitions correctly.	Consistently moves to the beat of the music.
3	Usually performs patterns and transitions correctly.	Usually moves to the beat of the music.
2	Sometimes performs patterns and transitions correctly.	Sometimes moves to the beat of the music.
1	Seldom performs patterns and transitions correctly.	Seldom moves to the beat of the music.
0	Violates safety procedures and/or does not complete the assessment task.	

Consistently = 90% and above

Usually = 75% - 89%

Sometimes = 50% -74%

Seldom = below 50%

■ Assessment Protocols:

Directions for Students (Read aloud, verbatim):

- Today, I'm going to look at your dance sequence.
- When the music starts, begin the dance and continue until the music stops.
- Stay inside the square.
- Show me your best dance by performing each step correctly, with smooth transitions and to the beat of the music.
- Don't stop until the music stops.

Directions for Teachers:

Preparation:

- See the chapter titled Procedures to Administer & Score PE Metrics Assessments for instruction, warm-up, camera location and operation.
- Six students can be assessed at one time within a 20-foot x 20-foot square performance area.
- Repeat the dance as many times as necessary to assess all children.

Safety:

- Be sure that students understand where to start and the boundaries of the performance area.
- Allow only safe footwear (no sandals, slides, boots, bare feet, etc.).
- If outside, use a smooth, hard surface that is free of obstructions.

Equipment/Materials:

- Use tape or 6 to 8 cones to form a 20-foot x 20-foot area.
- Teacher-selected music for grade-level-appropriate dance that uses 3 different step patterns.
- CD/cassette player.
- See Appendix A for grade-level-appropriate dance resources.

Diagram of Space/Distances:

△ = Cone

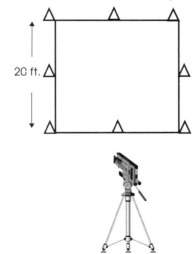

20 ft.

20 ft.

Camera Location and Operation:

Set up camera outside cones so that entire performance area can be viewed. The students' entire bodies, including the feet, must be in view and close enough to assess the patterns.

Assessment Score Sheet

PE Teacher _____ Grade _____ Date _____

School _____ Classroom Teacher _____

Student Name	ID Number	Gender	Patterns & Transitions (0-4)	Beat of the Music (0-4)	Total Score (0-8) 6=Competence

Dribble With Hand & Jog

Grade 2

Standard 1:

Demonstrates competency in motor skills and movement patterns needed to perform a variety of physical activities.

Performance Indicator:

Dribble, kick, throw, catch and strike a ball.

Assessment Task:

Dribble a ball with one hand to a cone and back while jogging slowly.

Criteria for Competence (Level 3):

1. Dribbles with selected essential elements:
   a) pushing action of finger pads.
   b) ball at approximately waist height.
   c) ball in front of body and to the "dribble hand" side of the midline.
2. Maintains a slow jog, with some variation in speed, while dribbling the designated distance.
3. Maintains a continuous dribble within the boundaries.

■ Assessment Rubric:

Level	1. Form	2. Space & Distance	3. Ball Control
4	Displays all the selected essential elements, with fluid motion.	Maintains consistent speed throughout the task.	Maintains a smooth (no change in rhythm), continuous dribble within the boundaries.
3	Dribbles with selected essential elements: a) pushing action of finger pads. b) ball at approx. waist height. c) ball in front of body and to the "dribble hand" side of the midline.	Maintains a slow jog, with some variation in speed, while dribbling the designated distance.	Maintains a continuous dribble within the boundaries.
2	Dribbles with 2 of 3 essential elements present.	Fails to maintain the jog or walks part of the designated distance.	Stops dribbling **or** ball goes outside the boundaries.
1	Dribbles with only 1 essential element present.	Does not jog while dribbling the designated distance.	Stops dribbling **and** ball goes outside the boundaries.
0	Violates safety procedures and/or does not complete the assessment task.		

Note: Control of ball and body is very important as children begin to travel at a rate higher than walking. The differences are often seen in walking versus jogging and being able to control ball and body to circle the cone and stop at finish/starting line.

■ Assessment Protocols:

Directions for Students (Read aloud, verbatim):

- Today, I'm going to look at how you dribble while jogging.
- Stand behind the starting line.
- On my signal, dribble the ball down to the large cone while you jog slowly and stay within your own lane.
- Dribble around the cone while jogging and back to the starting line.
- This is not a race.
- We are looking to see if you show good dribbling form by using your finger pads to push the ball, keeping the ball in front of you about waist height and keeping the ball to the front and "dribble hand" side of your body, while you maintain a slow jog with good control.
- Keep dribbling and jogging until you return to the starting line.

Directions for Teachers:

Preparation:

- See the chapter titled Procedures to Administer & Score PE Metrics Assessments for instruction, warm-up, camera location and operation.
- Clearly indicate the starting/finish line, lane area and turning point.

Safety:

- Be sure that students understand where the starting/finish line and turning cone are located.
- Allow only safe footwear (no sandals, slides, boots, bare feet, etc.).
- If outside, use a smooth, hard surface that is free of obstructions.

Equipment/Materials:

- 1 adequately inflated 10- or 12-inch playground ball.
- 8 small cones to form lane.
- 1 large cone to turn around.
- Floor tape to form the starting/finish line.

Diagram of Space/Distances:

Use cones to form a lane 5 feet wide and 30 feet long, with an additional 10 feet of unobstructed space behind the starting/finish line and 10 feet beyond the turning point (total of 50 feet). Cones should be placed down each lane line 10 feet apart to mark the lane lines. One large cone placed in middle of lane at 30 feet from starting/finish line will indicate the turn-around mark.

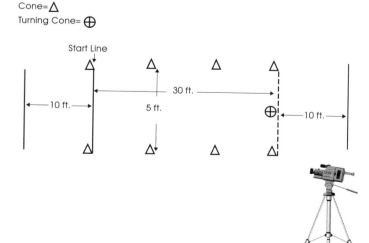

Camera Location and Operation:

Set up camera at turning zone but outside cones, so that student can be viewed dribbling into and making the turn. The student's entire body, including the feet, must be in view and close enough to assess the form.

Assessment Score Sheet

PE Teacher _____   Grade _____   Date _____

School _____   Classroom Teacher _____

Student Name	ID Number	Gender	Form (0-4)	Speed & Distance (0-4)	Control (0-4)	Total Score (0-12) 9=Competent

2 Grade
Galloping

Standard 1:

Demonstrates competency in motor skills and movement patterns needed to perform a variety of physical activities.

Performance Indicator:

Demonstrates a mature pattern of jumping, galloping, sliding and skipping.

Assessment Task:

Gallop continuously for 30 feet, with one foot leading. Repeat the task with the other foot leading.

Criteria for Competence (Level 3):

1. Gallops with the essential elements of a mature pattern:

   a) same foot leading.

   b) forward orientation.

   c) moment of non-support.

   d) back foot does not move in front of lead foot.

2. Gallops with no break in action for 30 feet, turns and gallops back to the start, with the other foot leading.

■ Assessment Rubric:

Level	1. Form	2. Consistency
4	Displays all the essential elements of a mature pattern, with fluid motion for entire task.	Gallops smoothly, with continuous action with each foot leading.
3	Gallops with the essential elements of a mature pattern for entire task: a) same foot leading. b) forward orientation. c) moment of non-support. d) back foot does not move in front of lead foot.	Gallops with no break in action for 30 feet, turns and gallops back to the start, with the other foot leading.
2	Gallops with only 3 of 4 essential elements present.	Gallops with no more than 1 break in action for entire task, turns and gallops back to the start, with other foot leading.
1	Gallops with 2 or fewer essential elements present.	Two or more breaks in action and/or does not return to the start with the other foot leading.
0	Violates safety procedures and/or does not complete the assessment task.	

■ **Assessment Protocols:**

Directions for Students (Read aloud, verbatim):

- Today, I'm going to look at your galloping.
- Stand behind the starting line.
- On my signal, gallop to the end of the lane, with one foot leading.
- Stop, then turn around and gallop back, with the other foot leading.
- Stay in your lane.
- This is not a race.
- Show me your best galloping form by using the same foot to lead, facing forward, bringing your feet together without crossing them and without stopping your movement.

Directions for Teachers:

Preparation:

- See the chapter titled Procedures to Administer & Score PE Metrics Assessments for instruction, warm-up, camera location and operation.
- Clearly indicate the lane area and stopping zones.
- Remind students to switch lead feet once they reach the stopping line, for the return.
- Then, same student turns around and gallops back, with other foot leading.
- Do not designate right foot or left foot. Use terms "one foot" and "the other foot."

Safety:

- Be sure that students understand where the start and end of the lane are located.
- Allow only safe footwear (no sandals, boots, bare feet, etc.).
- If outside, use a smooth, hard surface that is free of obstructions.

Equipment/Materials:

- At least 8 cones to form lane.
- Floor tape to form starting and finish line.

Diagram of Space/Distances:

Use cones to form a lane 5 feet wide and 30 feet long, with an additional 10 feet of unobstructed space beyond both the starting and finish lines (total of 50 feet long). Cones placed on each side of lane no more than 10 feet apart.

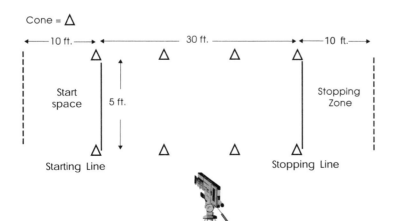

Camera Location and Operation:

Set up camera outside cones, so that student can be viewed galloping from the side. The student's entire body, including the feet, must be in view and close enough to assess the form.

Assessment Score Sheet

PE Teacher _____ Grade _____ Date _____

School _____ Classroom Teacher _____

Student Name	ID Number	Gender	Form (0-4)	Consistency (0-4)	Total Score (0-8) 6=Competent

Standard 1:

Demonstrates competency in motor skills and movement patterns needed to perform a variety of physical activities.

Performance Indicator:

Create and perform a gymnastics sequence.

Assessment Task:

Combine balancing, transferring weight and rolling actions into a sequence.

Criteria for Competence (Level 3):

1. Includes a momentary still beginning and ending.
2. Two balances are performed and held for 3 seconds.
3. Two different weight transfers are performed with good technique, one of which must be a roll.

■ Assessment Rubric:

Level	1. Still Beginning & End	2. Balances	3. Weight Transfer
4	Still beginning and end are held, with very clear shapes.	Both balances are held for 3 seconds, with good extensions.	Two different weight transfers are performed smoothly, with fluid motion throughout the sequence. One transfer is a roll.
3	Includes a momentary still beginning and ending.	Two balances are performed and held for 3 seconds.	Two different weight transfers are performed, with good technique, one of which must be a roll.
2	Beginning or ending is not still.	Two balances are performed, but only 1 is held for 3 seconds.	One weight transfer is performed with good technique.
1	Beginning and ending are not still.	Does not perform 2 balances or hold either for 3 seconds.	Neither weight transfer used good technique.
0	Violates safety procedures and/or does not complete the assessment task.		

■ **Assessment Protocols:**

Directions for Students (Read aloud, verbatim):

- Today, I'm going to look at the gymnastics sequence you practiced.
- Perform your sequence the way you wrote it on your paper.
- Your sequence should include 2 different balances held for 3 seconds each and 2 different transfers of body weight, 1 of which is a roll (may be an egg roll or shoulder roll).
- We will be looking to see if you start your sequence in a still position and end it in a still position, and if you include all the parts of your sequence and perform your sequence smoothly.
- Start inside the rectangle and do your entire sequence inside that rectangle.

Directions for Teachers:

Preparation:

- See the chapter titled Procedures to Administer & Score PE Metrics Assessments for instruction, warm-up, camera location and operation.
- Students should have designed the sequence during previous lessons and recorded the sequence on paper.
- Students should have memorized and practiced the sequence until it is repeatable.
- Clearly indicate the 10-foot x 20-foot rectangular performance area.

Safety:

- Students should perform forward or backward rolls only when they are ready. (Egg roll or shoulder roll meets the criteria.)
- Be sure that students understand where to start and know the boundaries of the performance area.
- Allow only safe footwear (no sandals, slides, boots, etc.).
- If outside, use a smooth surface that is free of obstructions, and provide appropriate mats where needed.

Equipment/Materials:

- As many mats as necessary.

Diagram of Space/Distances:

The performance area should be limited to a 10-foot X 20-foot rectangle. You may use the floor, a floor exercise or wrestling mat, a sequence of mats or a combination of mats and a designated space on the floor (within camera view).

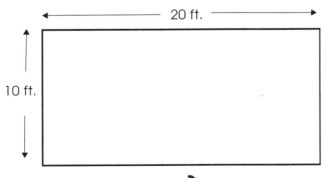

Camera Location and Operation:

The camera must be able to see the performer during the entire routine.
A side view of the performer is best.

Assessment Score Sheet

PE Teacher _____   Grade _____   Date _____

School _____   Classroom Teacher _____

Student Name	ID Number	Gender	Beginning and Ending (0-4)	Balances (0-4)	Weight Transfer (0-4)	Total Score (0-12) 9=Competent

2 Grade
Jump Forward

Standard 1:

Demonstrates competency in motor skills and movement patterns needed to perform a variety of physical activities.

Performance Indicator:

Demonstrates a mature pattern of jumping, galloping, sliding and skipping.

Assessment Task:

Jump forward, using a two-foot take off and a two-foot landing.

Criteria for Competence (Level 3):

1. Jumps with the essential elements of a mature pattern:

   a) arms back and knees bent in preparation.

   b) 2-foot simultaneous take-off.

   c) swings arms forward to at least shoulder height.

   d) 2-foot simultaneous landing.

   e) knees bend on landing.

   F) jumps with one continuous motion.

2. Jumps with sufficient force to propel the body forward at least 3 feet without falling backward.

■ Assessment Rubric:

Level	1. Form	2. Distance
4	Displays all the essential elements of a mature pattern, with fluid motion.	Jumps with smooth, balanced action, traveling forward at least 3 feet without falling backward.
3	Jumps with the essential elements of a mature pattern: a) arms back and knees bent in preparation. b) 2-foot simultaneous take-off. c) swings arms forward to at least shoulder height. d) 2-foot simultaneous landing. e) knees bend on landing. f) jumps with one continuous motion.	Jumps with sufficient force to propel the body forward at least 3 feet without falling backward.
2	Jumps with 5 of 6 essential elements.	Fails to jump forward at least 3 feet **or** falls backward on landing.
1	Jumps with 4 or fewer essential elements.	Fails to jump forward at least 3 feet **and** falls backward on landing.
0	Violates safety procedures and/or does not complete the assessment task.	

Note: Toes must be behind the starting line prior to the jump, and feet must clear the jumping line completely when landing.

■ Assessment Protocols:

Directions for Students (Read aloud, verbatim):

- Today, I'm going to look at your jumping.
- Stand behind the starting line.
- On my signal, you will jump forward at least 3 feet, using a 2-foot take-off and a 2-foot landing, without falling backward.
- Your feet must land over the "jumping line."
- Then, step back to your starting spot.
- Wait for the 'jump when ready' signal each time.
- This is not a contest to see who can jump the farthest.
- Show me your best jumping form by starting with your arms back and knees bent, jumping from 2 feet at the same time as you bring your arms forward as high as your shoulders, and land on 2 feet with a bend in your knees.
- Jump with one continuous motion.
- You will do 3 jumps.

Directions to Teachers:

Preparation

- See the chapter titled Procedures to Administer & Score PE Metrics Assessments for instruction, warm-up, camera location and operation.
- Three students can be assessed at one time.
- Clearly indicate the starting and jumping lines.
- If necessary, reiterate that this is not a contest to see who can jump the farthest.

Safety:

- Be sure that students understand where their starting spot is located.
- Allow only safe footwear (no sandals, slides, boots, bare feet, etc.).
- If outside, use a smooth, hard surface that is free of obstructions.

Equipment/Materials:

- Tape for 2 lines on floor at least 10 feet long.
- 3 spots marked on the starting line.

Diagram of Space/Distances:

Mark 3 spots on the starting line to indicate where students should start. Place the jumping line 3 feet away.

S=Student

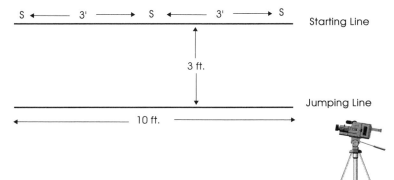

Camera Location and Operation:

Set up camera at an angle in front of and at the end of the jumping line. It must be far enough away so that all 3 students can be viewed while jumping at the same time. The jumping line and the students' entire bodies, including the feet, must be in view and close enough to assess the form.

Assessment Score Sheet

PE Teacher _____   Grade _____   Date _____

School _____   Classroom Teacher _____

Student Name	ID Number	Gender	Form (0-4)			Distance (0-4)			Total Score (0-24) 18=Competent
			1st	2nd	3rd	1st	2nd	3rd	

Jumping & Landing Combination

Standard 1:

Demonstrates competency in motor skills and movement patterns needed to perform a variety of physical activities.

Performance Indicator:

Jump and land in various combinations (1 to same foot, 1 to the other foot, 1 to 2 feet, 2 to 2 feet, 2 to 1 foot).

Assessment Task:

From a walk or jog, jump onto a box with a 1-foot take-off, landing on 2 feet, and jump down from the box using a 2-foot take-off and landing on 2 feet.

Criteria for Competence (Level 3):

1. Jumping onto a box:

   a) makes a smooth transition into the 1-foot take-off.

   b) uses a 1-foot take-off.

   c) uses a 2-foot landing on the box.

   d) jumps to a controlled position on top of the box.

2. Jumping off of the box:

   a) uses a 2-foot take-off.

   b) uses a 2-foot landing.

   c) absorbs the force of the landing through the feet, knees and hips.

   d) jumps to a controlled landing.

■ Assessment Rubric:

Level	1. Jump Onto the Box	2. Jump Off of the Box
4	Displays all the selected essential elements, with fluid motion.	Jumps with smooth, balanced action.
3	Jumps on to box, with selected criteria: a) makes a smooth transition into the 1-foot take-off. b) uses a 1-foot take-off. c) uses a 2-foot landing on the box. d) jumps to a controlled position on top of the box.	Jumps off box with selected criteria: a) uses a 2-foot take-off. b) uses a 2-foot landing. c) absorbs force of the landing through the feet, knees and hips. d) jumps to a controlled landing.
2	Jumps with 3 essential elements present.	Jumps with 3 essential elements present.
1	Jumps with 2 or fewer essential elements present.	Jumps with 2 or fewer essential elements present.
0	Violates safety procedures and/or does not complete the assessment task.	

■ **Assessment Protocols:**

Directions for Students (Read aloud, verbatim):

- Today, I am going to look at your jumping and landing form.

  Begin on the starting line. Walk or jog to the box, and jump from one foot onto the box, landing on 2 feet in a controlled position.

- You then will jump down from the box, using a 2-foot take-off to a 2-foot landing.

- Remember, 1 foot to 2, then 2 feet to 2. We will be looking to see if you can smoothly go into your 1-to 2-foot jump and pause and then make a good 2-foot jump with a controlled landing.

- Again, you must take off from only 1 foot and land with 2 feet on the box. Take off from the box on 2 feet and land on 2 feet.

Directions for Teachers:

Preparation:

- See the chapter titled Procedures to Administer & Score PE Metrics Assessments for instruction, warm-up, camera location and operation.

- Assess one student at a time.

- Allow students to jump when they are ready.

Safety:

- Use stable boxes/low bench or mats (that do not tip or slide).

- Allow only safe footwear (no sandals, slides, boots, bare feet, etc.).

- If outside, use a smooth, hard surface that is free of obstructions.

Equipment/Materials:

- 1 jumping box/low benches or mat (12 inches high)

- 1 landing mat.

Diagram of Space/Distances:

Place a starting line 5 feet from the box. Place mat next to the box for landing. Set up the camera so that you can see the start and mat landing for the student being tested.

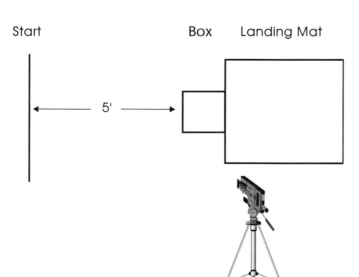

Start   Box   Landing Mat

← 5' →

Camera Location and Operation:

Set up camera to the side of the box the student is jumping onto. The student's entire body, including the feet, must be in view and close enough to assess the form. The camera should be placed so that you can see the beginning and end of each student's performance.

Assessment Score Sheet

PE Teacher _____   Grade _____   Date _____

School _____   Classroom Teacher _____

Student Name	ID Number	Gender	Jump on to the Box (0-4)	Jump off of the Box (0-4)	Total Score (0-8) 6=Competent

2 Grade
Locomotor Sequence

Standard 1 :
Demonstrates competency in motor skills and movement patterns needed to perform a variety of physical activities.

Performance Indicator:
Combine hopping, jumping, galloping, sliding and skipping into locomotor sequences.

Assessment Task:
Perform a sequence of 3 locomotor movements (hop, jump, gallop, slide, skip), with smooth transitions between each locomotor movement.

Criteria for Competence (Level 3):
1. Performs 3 locomotor movements with mature patterns.
2. Transitions between locomotor movements are smooth.

■ Assessment Rubric:

Level	1. Locomotor Pattern	2. Transitions
4	Performs 3 locomotor movements, with mature patterns and fluid motion.	Smooth fluid transitions throughout the sequence.
3	Performs 3 locomotor movements with mature patterns.	Transitions between locomotor movements are smooth.
2	Performs 2 of 3 locomotor movements with mature patterns.	One transition is not smooth.
1	Performs 1 or no locomotor movements with a mature pattern.	More than one transition is not smooth.
0	Violates safety procedures and/or does not complete the assessment task.	

■ Assessment Protocols:

Directions for Students (Read aloud, verbatim):

- Today, I'm going to look at the locomotor sequence you wrote down to perform.
- Start behind the starting line.
- Perform your sequence the way you wrote it on your paper.
- Stay in your lane.
- We are looking to see if you can perform your sequence using 3 locomotor movements with good form and two smooth transitions.
- Begin with one locomotor skill. When you reach the second set of cones, change to another skill. When you reach the third set of cones, change to your final skill.

Directions for Teachers:

Preparation

- See the chapter titled Procedures to Administer & Score PE Metrics Assessments for instruction, warm-up, camera location and operation.
- Clearly indicate the 5-foot X 45-foot performance strip and where the change cones are located.
- Students should have memorized and practiced the sequence until it is repeatable.

Safety:

- Be sure that students understand where to start and know the boundaries of the performance area.
- Allow only safe footwear (no sandals, slides, boots, bare feet, etc.).
- If outside, use a smooth, hard surface that is free of obstructions.

Equipment/Materials:

- Tape or 6 cones to form a 5-foot X 45-foot performance strip.

Diagram of Space/Distances:

Create a 5-foot X 45-foot area in which student performs sequence.

Cone =

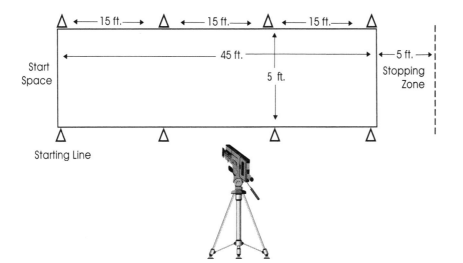

Camera Location and Operation:

Set up camera near middle of rectangular strip outside the cones, so that entire performance area can be viewed. The student's entire body, including the feet, must be in view and close enough to assess the form. Move the camera focus to be able to keep the student in the center of the picture during the whole sequence.

Assessment Score Sheet

PE Teacher _____   Grade _____   Date _____

School _____   Classroom Teacher _____

Student Name	ID Number	Gender	Locomotor Patterns (0-4)	Transitions (0-4)	Total Score (0-8) 6=Competent

Overhand Catching

Standard 1:

Demonstrates competency in motor skills and movement patterns needed to perform a variety of physical activities.

Performance Indicator:

Dribble, kick, throw, catch and strike a ball.

Assessment Task:

Catch a ball tossed by the teacher, using an overhand catching pattern.

Criteria for Competency (Level 3):

1. Attempts the catch with selected essential elements:

   a) hands reach to meet the ball.

   b) only hands contact the ball.

   c) correct overhand catching pattern (thumbs "in").

   d) "gives" with the ball.

2. Catches the ball successfully.

■ Assessment Rubric:

Level	1. Form	2. Catches the Ball
4	Display all the selected essential elements, with fluid motion.	Catches the ball, with smooth action.
3	Attempts the catch with selected essential elements: a) hands reach to meet the ball. b) only hands contact the ball. c) correct overhand catching pattern (thumbs "in"). d) "gives" with the ball.	Catches the ball successfully.
2	Attempts the catch with 3 of 4 essential elements present.	Catches the ball but then juggles the ball and recovers it.
1	Attempts the catch with 2 or fewer essential elements present.	Fails to catch the ball or catches then drops it.
0	Violates safety procedures and/or does not complete the assessment task.	

Note: "Attempts the catch" is used so that student is given credit for mechanics regardless of success of catch. Success is measured in the "Catches the Ball" category.

■ Assessment Protocols:

Directions for Students (Read aloud, verbatim):

- Today, I'm going to look at your overhand catch.
- Start on your spot, but you don't have to stay there to catch the ball.
- I will toss a ball to you.
- Show me your best overhand catching form by having your hands in ready position, reaching for the ball using only your hands with your thumbs facing in, and giving with the ball.
- You will have 3 tries.

Directions for Teachers:

Preparation

- See the chapter titled Procedures to Administer & Score PE Metrics Assessments for instruction, warm-up, camera location and operation.
- Clearly indicate where student should stand (15 feet from teacher).
- Use a gentle underhand toss that delivers the ball to the student between chest and head height.
- If the toss is poor, you may repeat the toss after verbally indicating on the video that the toss will be repeated.

Safety:

- Set up catching area so that no other students can enter it.

Equipment/Materials:

- 4 playground balls (size 8-10 inches).
- 2 spots marked on floor.

Diagram of Space/Distances:

Mark two spots on the floor 15 feet apart. Teacher stands on one and student on the other spot. Student faces away from any distractions.

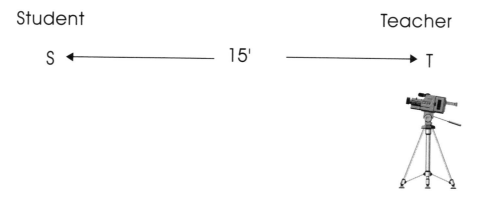

Student   Teacher

S ←——————— 15' ———————→ T

Camera Location and Operation:

Set up camera beside the teacher so that it points directly toward the student. The student's entire body, including the feet, must be in view and close enough to assess the form.

Assessment Score Sheet

PE Teacher _____ Grade _____ Date _____

School _____ Classroom Teacher _____

Student Name Ball	ID Number	Gender	Form (0-4)			Catches the (0-4)			Total Score (0-24) 18=Competent
			1st	2nd	3rd	1st	2nd	3rd	

2 Grade
Skipping

Standard 1:

Demonstrates competency in motor skills and movement patterns needed to perform a variety of physical activities.

Performance Indicator:

Demonstrates a mature pattern of jumping, galloping, sliding and skipping.

Assessment Task:

Skip continuously for 30 feet.

Criteria for Competence (Level 3):

1. Skips with the essential elements of a mature pattern:

    a) step-hop action on alternating feet.

    b) moment of non-support.

2. Skips a distance of 30 feet with no breaks in movement or loss of balance.

■ Assessment Rubric:

Level	1. Form	2. Consistency
4	Displays all the essential elements of a mature pattern, with fluid motion.	Skips with smooth movement for 30 feet.
3	Skips with the essential elements of a mature pattern: a) step-hop action on alternating feet. b) moment of non-support.	Skips for 30 feet with no breaks in movement or loss of balance.
2	Skips with 1 of 2 essential elements present.	Skips for 30 feet with no more than 1 break in movement or loss of balance.
1	Lacks the essential elements of skipping.	Skips for less than 30 feet, or with 2 or more breaks in movement, or loses balance.
0	Violates safety procedures and/or does not complete the assessment task.	

■ **Assessment Protocols:**

Directions for Students (Read aloud, verbatim):

- Today, I'm going to look at your skipping.
- Stand behind the starting line.
- Skip from the starting line to the finish line, while staying in your lane.
- This is not a race.
- Show me your best skipping form by using a step-hop action with alternating feet and no breaks in the movement.
- On my signal, skip to the finish line.

Directions for Teachers:

Preparation

- See the chapter titled Procedures to Administer & Score PE Metrics Assessments for instruction, warm-up, camera location and operation.
- Clearly indicate the lane area and finish line.

Safety:

- Be sure that students understand where the finish line is located.
- Allow only safe footwear (no sandals, boots, bare feet, etc.).
- If outside, use a smooth, hard surface that is free of obstructions.

Equipment/Materials:

- At least 8 cones to form lane.
- Mark the floor to form starting line and finish line.

Diagram of Space/Distances:

Use cones to form a lane 5 feet wide and 30 feet long with an additional 10 feet of unobstructed space beyond both the starting and finish lines (total of 50 feet long). Cones placed on each side of lane 10 feet apart.

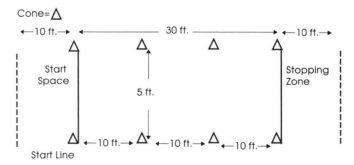

Camera Location and Operation:

Set up camera near end of lane but outside cones, so that student can be viewed the entire 30 feet. The student's entire body, including feet, must be in view and close enough to assess form.

Assessment Score Sheet

PE Teacher _____ Grade _____ Date _____

School _____ Classroom Teacher _____

Student Name	ID Number	Gender	Form (0-4)	Consistency (0-4)	Total Score (0-8) 6=Competent

Standard 1:

Demonstrates competency in motor skills and movement patterns needed to perform a variety of physical activities.

Performance Indicator:

Dribble, kick, throw, catch and strike a ball.

Assessment Task:

Strike a ball upward 5 times consecutively with a short-handled paddle.

Criteria for Competence (Level 3):

1. Strikes the ball for 5 continuous hits.
2. Does not move outside the 10-foot square.

■ Assessment Rubric:

Level	1. Success	2. Control
4	Strikes the ball for more than 5 continuous hits.	Very little travel from the starting position.
3	Strikes the ball for 5 continuous hits.	Does not move outside the 10-foot square.
2	Strikes for 3 or 4 continuous hits.	Moves outside the boundaries 1 or 2 times within the timeframe.
1	Strikes for 1 hit or 2 continuous hits.	Moves outside the boundaries 3 or more times within the timeframe.
0	Violates safety procedures and/or does not complete the assessment task.	

■ **Assessment Protocols:**

Directions for Students (Read aloud, verbatim):

- Today, I'm going to watch you striking a ball upward.
- You will have 30 seconds to try as many times as you can to get 5 or more hits in a row.
- Stand in the center of your personal-space area and stay in your area.
- Try to strike the ball at least 5 times in a row, staying in your area.
- If the ball hits the floor, bring it to the center of your space and start again.

Directions for Teachers:

Preparation

- See the chapter titled Procedures to Administer & Score PE Metrics Assessments for instruction, warm-up, camera location and operation.
- Clearly indicate the personal-space area.
- The trial ends when the student has struck the ball 5 or more times consecutively **or** 30 seconds has elapsed, whichever occurs first.
- Have another ball available for student in case first ball gets away.

Safety:

- Be sure that students understand where their personal-space area is located.
- If outside, use a smooth, hard surface that is free of obstructions.

Equipment/Materials:

- Short wooden or plastic paddle (not a racket with strings).
- Baseball-size or tennis ball-size soft foam ball.
- Floor tape or cones.
- Stopwatch or clock for timing 30 seconds.

Diagram of Space/Distances:

Mark a 10-foot x 10-foot square by using tape or cones.

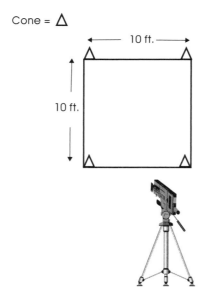

Cone = △

10 ft.

10 ft.

Camera Location and Operation:

Set up camera in front of the student and far enough away so that the entire personal space area can be viewed. The student's entire body, including the feet, must be in view and close enough to assess the form.

Assessment Score Sheet

PE Teacher _____   Grade _____   Date _____

School _____   Classroom Teacher _____

Student Name	ID Number	Gender	Success (0-4)	Control (0-4)	Total Score (0-8) 6=Competent

Grade
Basketball: Defense 5

Standard 1:

Demonstrates competency in motor skills and movement patterns needed to perform a variety of physical activities.

Performance Indicator:

Use defensive skills to gain possession of an object in a 2-on-1 situation.

Assessment Task:

Gain possession of a basketball in a 2-on-1 situation.

Criteria for Competence: (Level 3)

1. Usually assumes defensive stance while guarding:

    a) wide base of support.

    b) hands in a ready position.

2. Usually moves to block off the passing lane.

3. Usually plays aggressive defense by intercepting or making passing difficult for the offensive players.

■ Assessment Rubric:

Level	1. Defensive Stance	2. Blocks Passing Lanes	3. Aggressive Defense
4	Consistently assumes defensive stance while guarding.	Consistently moves to block off the passing lane.	Consistently plays aggressive defense by intercepting or making passing difficult for the offensive players.
3	Usually assumes defensive stance while guarding: a) wide base of support. b) hands in a ready position.	Usually moves to block off the passing lane.	Usually plays aggressive defense by intercepting or making passing difficult for the offensive players.
2	Sometimes assumes defensive stance while guarding.	Sometimes moves to block off the passing lane.	Sometimes plays aggressive defense by intercepting or making passing difficult for the offensive players.
1	Seldom assumes defensive stance while guarding.	Seldom moves to block off the passing lane.	Seldom plays aggressive defense by intercepting or making passing difficult for the offensive players.
0	Violates safety procedures and/or does not complete the assessment task.		

Consistently = 90% and above

Usually = 75% - 89%

Sometimes = 50% -74%

Seldom = below 50%

■ Assessment Protocols:

Directions for Students (Read aloud, verbatim):

- You will try to gain possession of a basketball against 2 offensive players, who will attempt to keep the ball away from you.
- You will play for 1 minute.
- You will be assessed on your ability to:
  a) assume a good defensive stance while guarding by using a wide base of support and having your hands in a ready position.
  b) move to block off the passing lane.
  c) play aggressive defense by intercepting or making passing difficult for the offensive players.
- The offensive players will start the ball. If the defense gets the ball, give it back to the offense.

Directions for Teachers:

Preparation

- See the chapter titled Procedures to Administer & Score PE Metrics Assessments for instruction, warm-up, camera location and operation.
- Select several competent students to alternate as offensive players. Instruct offensive players to play aggressively.

Safety:

- Playing area must be dry and clean, with at least 3 feet of clear space beyond the boundary line.

Equipment:

- Marked playing area (30 feet X 30 feet).
- Youth basketball.
- Stopwatch.

Diagram of space/distance:

O = Offensive Player   D = Defensive Player

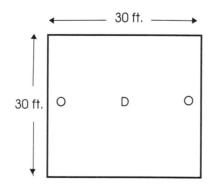

Camera Location/Operation:

The camera should be placed at a corner with sufficient distance to see all boundary lines within the viewing screen.

Assessment Score Sheet

PE Teacher _____   Grade _____   Date _____

School _____   Classroom Teacher _____

Student Name	ID Number	Gender	Defensive Stance (0-4)	Block Passing Lane (0-4)	Aggressive Defense (0-4)	Total Score (0-12) 9=Competent

5 Grade
Basketball: Dribble, Pass & Receive

Standard 1:

Demonstrates competency in motor skills and movement patterns needed to perform a variety of physical activities.

Performance Indicator:

Dribble, pass and receive a ball with a partner.

Assessment Task:

Dribble, pass and receive a basketball while traveling at a jog.

Criteria for Competence (Level 3):

1. Dribbles with control while moving at a slow, consistent jog.
2. Sends a catchable* lead pass to partner so it can be caught outside the passing lane without a break in the receiver's stride on at least 3 passes.
3. Moves forward outside the passing lane to meet the ball and catches 3 catchable passes.

◾ Assessment Rubric:

Level	1. Dribbling	2. Passing	3. Receiving
4	Dribbles with consistent rhythm and control while moving at a slow, consistent jog.	Sends a catchable lead pass to partner so it can be caught outside the passing lane without a break in the receiver's stride on all passes.	Moves forward outside the passing lane to meet the ball and catches 4 catchable passes.
3	Dribbles with control while moving at a slow, consistent jog.	Sends a catchable lead pass to a partner so it can be caught outside the passing lane without a break in the receiver's stride on at least 3 passes.	Moves forward outside the passing lane to meet the ball and catches 3 catchable passes.
2	Dribbles with control while moving at an inconsistent jog.	Sends a catchable lead pass to partner so it can be caught outside the passing lane without a break in the receiver's stride on at least 2 passes.	Moves forward to meet the ball and catches 2 catchable passes.
1	Dribbles with frequent lack of control and inconsistent jog.	Sends a catchable lead pass to partner so it can be caught outside the passing lane without a break in the receiver's stride on fewer than 2 passes.	Moves to meet the ball and catches fewer than 2 catchable passes.
0	Violates safety procedures and/or does not complete the assessment task.		

*as determined by the teacher

■ Assessment Protocols:

Directions for Students (Read aloud, verbatim, and provide visual demonstration without the ball):

- You and your partner will perform dribbling, passing using a chest or bounce pass, and receiving skills while traveling on the outside of a passing lane marked by polyspots.
- The first person with the ball will dribble a short distance and then pass to a partner. You need to get the ball to your partner ahead of him or her and outside the passing lane. The person receiving will receive the ball, dribble and then pass the ball back to the first person. If you need to move inside the passing lane to receive the ball, dribble it back to the outside of the passing lane before you pass it to your partner. Continue this pattern so that each person completes 2 passes and 2 receptions going toward the end line. When you reach the end line, turn around and repeat the passes/receptions coming back. Each partner will pass and catch the ball at least 4 times (2 going up, 2 coming back).
- You will be assessed on your ability to:
  a) Dribble with control while moving at a slow jog.
  b) Send a catchable lead pass to your partner.
  c) Move to meet the ball and catch a catchable pass.

Directions for Teachers:

Preparation

- See the chapter titled Procedures to Administer & Score PE Metrics Assessments for instruction, warm-up, camera location and operation.
- Students of relatively equal skill — determined by prior assessment — should be paired together.

Safety:

- Area should be free of obstructions.

Equipment:

- 8 polyspots   • Youth basketball

Diagram of space/distance:

Camera Location/Operation

The camera should be placed to the side of the end line so that the players can be viewed for the entire distance to be traveled. The beginning line should be seen at the top and the end line at the bottom of the viewing screen.

A=Player A-Starting position   B=Player B-Starting Position
▲=Polyspots mark passing lane (Passing lane=10 ft wide and approximately 60 ft long).
Path of Partner B= ——————
Path of Ball= - - - - - - - ▶
Path of Partner A= ▬ ▬ ▬
Starting Line= ▬▬▬▬

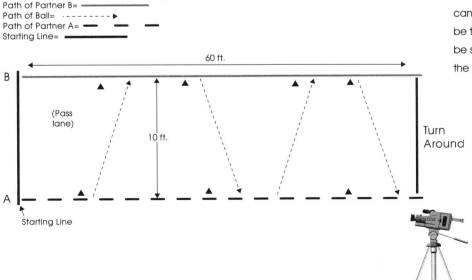

Assessment Score Sheet

PE Teacher _____   Grade _____   Date _____

School _____   Classroom Teacher _____

Student Name	ID Number	Gender	Dribbling (0-4)	Passing (0-4)	Receiving (0-4)	Total Score (0-12) 9=Competent

Basketball: Offense 5

Standard 1:

Demonstrates competency in motor skills and movement patterns needed to perform a variety of physical activities.

Performance Indicator:

Use offensive skills to maintain possession of an object in a 2-on-1 situation.

Assessment Task:

Maintain possession of a basketball in 2-on-1 situation against a defender.

Criteria for Competence: (Level 3)

1. Usually moves to open space to create a passing lane.
2. Usually sends a catchable lead pass to a partner.
3. Usually catches a catchable pass.

■ Assessment Rubric:

Level	1. Movement Without the Ball	2. Passing	3. Catching
4	Consistently moves to open space with good timing and a clear intent to create a passing lane.	Consistently anticipates partner's movement and sends a catchable leading pass to a partner.	Consistently catches a catchable pass.
3	Usually moves to open space to create a passing lane.	Usually sends a catchable lead pass to a partner.	Usually catches a catchable pass.
2	Sometimes moves to open space to create a passing lane.	Sometimes sends a catchable lead pass to a partner.	Sometimes catches a catchable pass, with an occasional bobble or drop.
1	Seldom moves to open space to create a passing lane.	Seldom sends a catchable lead pass to a partner.	Seldom catches a catchable pass.
0	Violates safety procedures and/or does not complete the assessment task.		

Consistently = 90% and above

Usually = 75% - 89%

Sometimes = 50% -74%

Seldom = below 50%

■ **Assessment Protocols:**

Directions for Students (Read aloud, verbatim):
- You will play a game of 2-on-1, with no dribbling, against a defender who will attempt to restrict, obstruct or intercept your passes. You and your partner will play 2-on-1 for 1 minute. A variety of passes may be used.
- You will be assessed on your ability to:
  a) Move without the ball to open space to create a passing lane.
  b) Lead your partner with a catchable pass.
  c) Catch catchable passes with control.
- You and your partner will take possession with a throw-in at the beginning, after an interception and if the ball goes out of bounds.

Directions for Teachers:

Preparation
- See the chapter titled Procedures to Administer & Score PE Metrics Assessments for instruction, warm-up, camera location and operation.
- Students of relatively equal skill — determined by prior assessment — should be paired together.
- Select several skilled students to alternate as the defensive player. Instruct defender to moderately restrict, obstruct or intercept passes.

Safety:
- Playing area must be dry and clean with at least 3 feet of clear space beyond the boundary line.

Equipment:
- Marked playing area (30 feet X 30 feet) .
- Youth basketball.
- Pinnies of contrasting colors to which numbers will be attached to identify students on offense.
- Stopwatch.

Diagram of Space/Distance – Mark Camera Location

O = Offensive Player   D = Defensive Player

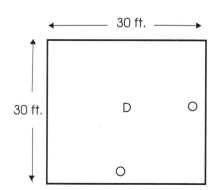

Camera Location/Operation:
The camera should be placed at a corner with sufficient distance to see all boundary lines within the viewing screen.

Assessment Score Sheet

PE Teacher _____ Grade _____ Date _____

School _____ Classroom Teacher _____

Student Name	ID Number	Gender	Movement without the Ball (0-4)	Passing (0-4)	Catching (0-4)	Total Score (0-12) 9=Competent

5 Dance
Grade

Standard 1:

Demonstrates competency in motor skills and movement patterns needed to perform a variety of physical activities.

Performance Indicator:

Perform a dance.

Assessment Task:

Perform the given steps and sequences to the beat of the music for an age-appropriate dance (e.g. line, square, folk, step, social).

Criteria for Competence (Level 3):

1. Consistently performs steps of the dance correctly.
2. Consistently performs sequences of the dance correctly.
3. Consistently moves to the beat of the music.

■ Assessment Rubric:

Level	1. Steps	2. Sequences	3. Beat of the Music
4	Always performs steps (movements, space, position) of the dance correctly.	Always performs sequences (movement sequences, order) of the dance correctly.	Always moves to the beat of the music.
3	Consistently performs steps of the dance correctly.	Consistently performs sequences of the dance correctly.	Consistently moves to the beat of the music.
2	Usually performs steps of the dance correctly.	Usually performs sequences of the dance correctly.	Usually moves to the beat of the music.
1	Sometimes or never performs steps of the dance correctly.	Sometimes or never performs sequences of the dance correctly.	Sometimes or never moves to the beat of the music.
0	Violates safety procedures and/or does not complete the assessment task.		

Always = no errors

Consistently = 90% or above

Usually = 75% - 89%

Sometimes or never = below 75%

■ **Assessment Protocols:**

Directions for Students (Read aloud, verbatim):
- You will perform a dance that we have learned and practiced.
- You will be assessed on your ability to:
    a) perform the steps of the dance.
    b) perform the sequences of the dance.
    c) consistently move to the beat of the music.
- Continue dance until the music stops.

Directions for Teachers:
Preparation
- See the chapter titled Procedures to Administer & Score PE Metrics Assessments for instruction, warm-up, camera location and operation.
- The teacher selects an age-appropriate dance from those that students have been taught and have practiced.
- The dance selected should be representative of the steps most common among the dances taught.
- Instrumental music is recommended unless verbal direction (as in square dance) is included on recording.
- Students should be spaced so that each can be seen clearly by the teacher and the camera.
- Group students with a partner or in a small group, as may be required for your dance.
- Continue music until the end of the "song," or play for 2 minutes.

Safety:
- Dance area is clean and dry, free from obstruction, with clear perimeter around the dance area.

Equipment:
- CD/Tape player.
- CD or tape.
- See Appendix A for grade-level-appropriate dances and resources.

Diagram of Space/Distance:

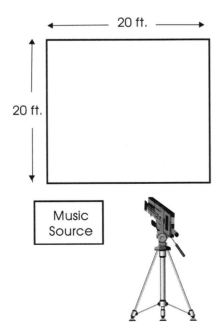

←——— 20 ft. ———→

20 ft.

Music Source

Camera Location/Operation:
The camera can be placed in front of the dancers so that all can be seen in the viewing screen. The music source must be close enough to the camera to that the music can also be recorded.

Assessment Score Sheet

PE Teacher _____   Grade _____   Date _____

School _____   Classroom Teacher _____

Student Name	ID Number	Gender	1. Steps (0-4)	2. Sequences (0-4)	3. Beat of the Music (0-4)	Total Score (0-12) 9=Competent

Standard 1:

Demonstrates competency in motor skills and movement patterns needed to perform a variety of physical activities.

Performance Indicator:

Dribble and shoot an object for a goal.

Assessment Task:

While jogging, continuously dribble a puck with a hockey stick through a zigzag obstacle course, and shoot for a goal.

Criteria for Competence (Level 3):

1. Dribbles the hockey puck with essential elements:

   a) grip of hockey stick with dominant hand lower, thumbs pointing to ground, hands apart.

   b) continuous dribble.

   c) uses both sides of stick.

   d) maintains slow jog.

2. Shoots using all essential elements:

   a) sets up for shot by trapping or controlling the puck.

   b) uses a push shot.

   c) follows through to target.

■ Assessment Rubric:

Level	1. Dribble	2. Shoot
4	Displays all the essential elements with fluid motion.	Shoots using all the essential elements with fluid motion.
3	Dribbles the hockey puck with all essential elements: a) grip of hockey stick with dominant hand lower, thumbs pointing to ground, hands apart. b) continuous dribble.* c) uses both sides of stick. d) maintains slow jog.	Shoots using all the essential elements: a) sets up for shot by trapping or controlling the puck. b) uses a push shot. c) follows through to target.
2	Dribbles with 3 of 4 essential elements present.	Shoots using 2 of 3 essential elements.
1	Dribbles with 2 or fewer essential elements present.	Shoots using only 1 of 3 of the essential elements.
0	Violates safety procedures and/or does not complete the assessment task.	

*Puck should be kept within 4 feet of stick

■ Assessment Protocols:

Directions for Students (Read aloud, verbatim):

- Today, I'm going to watch you dribble and shoot for a goal using a hockey stick.
- Stand behind the starting line.
- On my signal, dribble the puck in and out of the 3 cones within the side boundaries while you jog slowly.
- Trap the puck when necessary to keep it from going outside the boundaries.
- This is not a race.
- When you reach the shooting line, first trap or control the puck, then shoot for the goal.
- Show me your best dribbling, trapping and shooting form.

Directions for Teachers:

Preparation

- See the chapter titled Procedures to Administer & Score PE Metrics Assessments for instruction, warm-up, camera location and operation.
- Clearly indicate the start, dribbling course, shooting line and goal.
- Assessment is 1 attempt.
- Intent of assessment is the dribble, trapping or controlling the puck, and shooting, not scoring a goal.

Safety:

- Set up course so that no other students can enter.
- Place goal near a wall so that shots do not interfere with other students.
- Allow only safe footwear (no sandals, boots, bare feet, etc.).
- If outside, use a smooth, hard surface that is free of obstructions.

Equipment/Materials:

- 1 hockey stick.
- 1 hockey puck.
- 6 cones.
- Tape for starting and shooting lines.
- Polyspots or tape for marking the sidelines.

Diagram of Space/Distances:

Place 3 cones 15 feet apart to form a course 10 feet wide and 50 feet long. The first cone is 10 feet from the start line and the last cone is 10 feet from the shooting line. Use 2 cones to make a 10-feet-wide goal 10 feet from the shooting line. Use polyspots or tape to mark the sidelines.

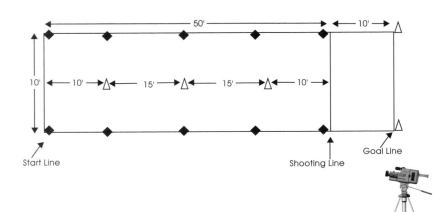

△ = Cones marking goal line and course

◆ = Polyspots marking sidelines

Camera Location and Operation:

Set up camera next to goal, so that student can be viewed dribbling, trapping and making the shot. The students' entire bodies, including the feet, must be in view and close enough to assess the form.

Assessment Score Sheet

PE Teacher _____   Grade _____   Date _____

School _____   Classroom Teacher _____

Student Name	ID Number	Gender	Dribble (0-4)	Shoot (0-4)	Total Score (0-8) 6=Competent

5 Gymnastics

Grade

Standard 1:

Demonstrates competency in motor skills and movement patterns needed to perform a variety of physical activities.

Performance Indicator:

Perform a gymnastics/movement sequence.

Assessment Task:

Perform a self-designed gymnastics/movement sequence with the following 7 components: (1) a starting shape, (2) roll, (3) transfer of weight from feet to hands, (4) balance, (5) leap or jump, (6) turn and (7) ending shape.

Criteria for Competence (Level 3):

1. Sequence includes at least 6 of the required components.
2. At least 5 of 7 components of the sequence are performed with good technique: clear beginning and ending shapes, still balances, controlled rolls, smooth weight transfers and strong leaps, jumps and turns.
3. Sequence includes smooth transitions between components with no more than 2 breaks in continuity.

■ Assessment Rubric:

Level	1. Composition	2. Technique	3. Transitions
4	Sequence includes all the required components.	Performs 6 of 7 components with good technique.	Sequence includes smooth transitions between components with no more than 1 break in continuity.
3	Sequence includes 6 of the required components.	Performs at least 5 of 7 components of the sequence with good technique: clear beginning and ending shapes, still balances, controlled rolls, smooth weight transfers, and strong leaps, jumps and turns.	Sequence includes smooth transitions between components with no more than 2 breaks in continuity.
2	Sequence includes 5 of the required components.	Only 4 of the components are performed with good technique.	Sequence includes transitions between components with no more than 3 breaks in continuity.
1	Sequence includes 4 or fewer of the required components.	Sequence includes 3 or fewer components performed with good technique.	Sequence includes 4 or more breaks in continuity.
0	Violates safety procedures and/or does not complete the assessment task.		

■ **Assessment Protocols:**

Directions for Teachers:

Preparation

- See the chapter titled Procedures to Administer & Score PE Metrics Assessments for instruction, warm-up, camera location and operation.

- It is recommended that written routines be submitted, reviewed and approved by the teacher prior to the assessment performance.

Safety:

- Performance area must be matted, sections taped, clean and dry, free from obstruction including at least a 5-foot clear perimeter.

- Students **must** wear clothing that neither restricts nor hinders movement.

- All jewelry that could potentially injure students, as well as objects in pockets, are to be removed.

Equipment:

- 20-foot X 20-foot tumbling mat. (If sections of mat are used, they must be taped together.)

- A different placement of mats may be used to accommodate the routine, facility or available mats (i.e., a long line of mats).

Diagram of Space/Distance

S = Student
M = Music Source

Camera Location/Operation:

The camera needs to be placed so that the entire performance of both performers can be seen. Camera placement will vary with mat placement and camera capability. For a 20-foot X 20-foot mat the best place for the camera will be in front (as shown) so that all corners of the area can be seen in the camera lens. For mats placed in a row, the best placement will be to the side of the mats so that the first and last mat can be seen within the camera angle and performers can be viewed slightly from the side.

Assessment Score Sheet

PE Teacher _____ Grade _____ Date _____

School _____ Classroom Teacher _____

Student Name	ID Number	Gender	Composition (0-4)	Technique (0-4)	Transition (0-4)	Total Score (0-12) 9=Competent

Standard 1:

Demonstrates competency in motor skills and movement patterns needed to perform a variety of physical activities.

Performance Indicator:

Perform sport specific skills for participation in individual non-competitive activities.

Assessment Task:

Inline skate on a level surface with changes in direction.

Criteria for Competence (Level 3):

1) Displays essential elements of forward stride without falling:
   a) short, continuous strokes.
   b) push sideward.
   c) glide through ready position.
   d) swing arms in opposition to foot stroke.
2) Displays essential elements of changing direction:
   a) glide through turn at consistent speed.
   b) look in direction of turn.
   c) lead with inside skate.

3) Displays essential elements of stopping:
   a) shoulders forward.
   b) weight on non-braking leg.
   c) slide brake foot forward with heel down and come to a complete stop.

■ Assessment Rubric:

Level	1. Forward Stride	2. Changing Direction	3. Stopping
4	Displays all essential elements of forward stride with fluid motion without falling.	Displays all essential elements of changing direction with fluid motion.	Displays all essential elements of stopping to come to a complete stop with good control.
3	Displays essential elements of forward stride without falling: a) short, continuous strokes. b) push sideward. c) glide through ready position. d) swing arms in opposition to foot stroke.	Displays essential elements of changing direction: a) glide through turn at consistent speed. b) look in direction of turn. c) lead with inside skate.	Displays essential elements of stopping: a) shoulders forward. b) weight on non-braking leg. c) slide brake foot forward with heel down and come to a complete stop.
2	Displays 3 of 4 essential elements of forward stride without falling.	Displays 2 of 3 essential elements of changing direction.	Displays 2 of 3 essential elements of stopping.
1	Displays 2 or fewer essential elements of forward stride and/or falls.	Displays 1 or no essential elements of changing direction.	Displays 1 or no essential elements of stopping and/or falls when stopping.
0	Violates safety procedures and/or does not complete the assessment task.		

■ Assessment Protocols:

Directions for Students (Read aloud, verbatim):

- You will skate the course as marked by the cones.
- You will be assessed on your ability to:
    - a) skate forward using short strokes, pushing sideward, gliding through ready position, swinging arms in opposition to foot stroke.
    - b) negotiate turn at consistent speed.
    - c) come to a complete stop within the stop zone, with shoulders forward, weight on non-braking leg, sliding brake foot forward with heel down.
- Use short, continuous strokes. No walking.
- You will go around the course twice.

Directions to Teachers: Preparation

- See the chapter titled Procedures to Administer & Score PE Metrics Assessments for instruction, warm-up, camera location and operation.
- Set up the course on a basketball court or smooth-surface parking lot, using cones to mark the starting, turning and stopping points.
- Students should use short, continuous strokes. No walking.

Safety:

- Properly fitting skates and safety equipment (helmet, and knee, wrist and elbow pads) must be worn by each student.
- Skate course must be clear of debris, holes and obstacles.
- All skates and safety equipment must be well-maintained and in good working order.

Equipment:

- Properly fitting skates and safety equipment (helmet, and knee, wrist and elbow pads) for each student.
- 8 cones to mark start line, stop zone, skating area and turning points .
- Arrows to be taped onto cones to mark direction each student is to skate through the course.

Diagram of Space/Distance

Course = 60 feet x 30 feet with 10 feet clear of end cones for turn
◆ = Cones

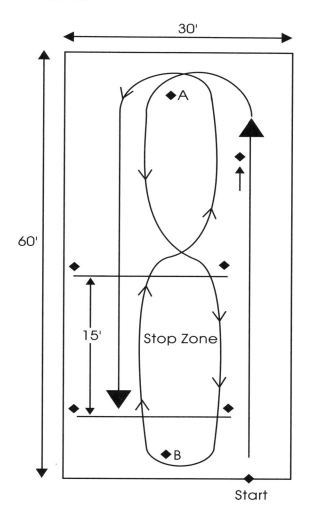

Travel in a Figure 8 pattern. Skate to Cone A and glide around to the left. On the return, cross over and glide around Cone B to the right. Return to Cone A and glide around Cone A again to the left. Skate to the Stop Zone and finish.

Camera Location/Operation:

Set the camera near the start/ stop zone so the stop zone can be viewed. The course and the student should be visible in the viewing screen so that performance can be clearly seen.

Assessment Score Sheet

PE Teacher _____   Grade _____   Date _____

School _____   Classroom Teacher _____

Student Name	ID Number	Gender	Forward Stride (0-4)	Changing Directions (0-4)	Stop (0-4)	Total Score (0-12) 9=Competent

Standard 1:

Demonstrates competency in motor skills and movement patterns needed to perform a variety of physical activities.

Performance Indicator:

Dribble, kick, throw, catch and strike a ball.

Assessment Task:

Use an overhand throwing pattern to send a ball to a large wall target.

Criteria for Competence (Level 3):

1. Throws a ball with selected essential elements:

   a) throwing elbow shoulder-high, hand back and side orientation in preparation for throw.

   b) trunk rotation, with elbow lagging behind hip.

   c) weight transfer to non-throwing forward foot.

2. Hits target area on wall.

■ Assessment Rubric:

Level	1. Form	2. Accuracy to Target
4	Displays all the selected essential elements with fluid motion and differentiated trunk rotation.	Hits target area on wall with force.
3	Throws with selected essential elements: a) throwing elbow shoulder-high, hand back and side orientation in preparation for the throw. b) trunk rotation, with elbow lagging behind hip. c) weight transfer to non-throwing forward foot.	Hits target area on wall.
2	Throws with 2 of 3 essential elements.	Hits wall but not target area.
1	Throws with 1 or no essential elements.	Ball fails to reach the wall.
0	Violates safety procedures and/or does not complete the assessment task.	

Note: Failure to use the overhand throwing pattern is scored as incomplete assessment task.

■ Assessment Protocols:

Directions for Students (Read aloud, verbatim):

- Today, I'm going to look at your overhand throw.
- You will be assessed on:
    a) having a side orientation.
    b) a good arm position.
    c) good trunk rotation.
    d) a step to your non-throwing forward foot.
    e) whether you hit the target.
- Stand behind the throwing line.
- You will have 3 trials.

Directions for Teachers:

Preparation

- See the chapter titled Procedures to Administer & Score PE Metrics Assessments for instruction, warm-up, camera location and operation.
- Clearly indicate the target square on the wall and the throwing line.

Safety:

- Set up throwing area so that no other students can enter it.

Equipment/Materials:

- Tennis balls.
- Tape to form throwing line and target square on a wall.

Diagram of Space/Distances:

Use tape to form a throwing line on the floor and a target square 6 feet x 6 feet on a wall 25 feet from the throwing line.

Place target square 3 feet off the floor.

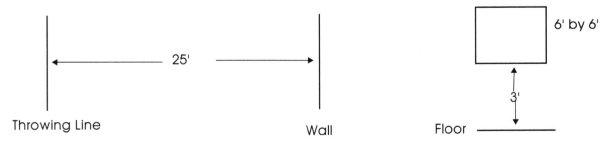

Throwing Line   Wall   Floor

25'   6' by 6'   3'

Camera Location and Operation:

Set up camera on same side as student's throwing arm. The student's entire body, including the feet, must be in view and close enough to assess the form. The camera placement should also allow the target on the wall to be seen in the picture.

Assessment Score Sheet

PE Teacher _____ Grade _____ Date _____

School _____ Classroom Teacher _____

Student Name	ID Number	Gender	Form (0-4)			Accuracy to Target (0-4)			Total Score (0-24) 18=Competent
			1st	2nd	3rd	1st	2nd	3rd	

5 Grade
Soccer: Dribble, Pass & Receive

Standard 1:

Demonstrates competence in motor skills and movement patterns needed to perform a variety of physical activities.

Performance Indicator:

Dribble, pass and receive a ball with a partner.

Assessment Task:

Dribble, pass and receive a soccer ball while traveling at a jog.

Criteria for Competence (Level 3):

1. Dribble with control while moving at a slow, consistent jog.
2. Sends a receivable lead pass to a partner so it can be received outside the passing lane without a break in the receiver's stride on at least 3 passes.
3. Moves forward and outside the passing lane to meet the ball while receiving at least 3 receivable passes.

■ Assessment Rubric:

Level	1. Dribbling	2. Passing	3. Receiving
4	Dribbles with consistent rhythm and control while moving at a slow, consistent jog.	Sends a receivable lead pass to a partner so it can be received outside the passing lane without a break in the receiver's stride on all 4 passes.	Moves forward and outside the passing lane to receive 4 receivable passes.
3	Dribbles with control while moving at a slow, consistent jog.	Sends a receivable lead pass to a partner so it can be received outside the passing lane without a break in the receiver's stride on at least 3 passes.	Moves forward and outside the passing lane to meet the ball while receiving at least 3 receivable passes.
2	Dribbles with control while moving at an inconsistent or slow speed.	Sends a receivable lead pass outside the passing lane to a partner so it can be received without a break in the receiver's stride on 2 passes.	Moves forward to receive at least 2 receivable passes.
1	Dribbles with frequent lack of control and/or inconsistent walking or jogging speed.	Sends a receivable lead pass outside the passing lane to a partner so it can be received without a break in the receiver's stride on fewer than 2 passes.	Moves to receive fewer than 2 receivable passes.
0	Violates safety procedures and/or does not complete the assessment task.		

■ **Assessment Protocols:**

Directions for Students (Read aloud, verbatim, and provide a visual demonstration without the ball):

- You and your partner will perform dribbling, passing and receiving skills while traveling on the outside of a passing lane marked by polyspots.

- The first person with the ball will dribble a short distance and then pass to a partner. You need to deliver the ball to your partner ahead of him or her and outside the passing lane. The person receiving the ball will dribble and then pass the ball back to the first person. Continue this pattern so that each person completes 2 passes and 2 receptions. If you need to move inside the passing lane to receive the ball, dribble it back to the outside of the passing lane before you pass it to your partner. When you reach the end line, turn around and repeat the passes coming back. Each of you will complete a total of at least 4 passes (2 going up, 2 coming back).

- You will be assessed on your ability to:

  a) Dribble with control while moving at a slow jog.

  b) Send a receivable lead pass to your partner.

  c) Move to receive a receivable pass.

Directions for Teachers:

Preparation

- See the chapter titled Procedures to Administer & Score PE Metrics Assessments for instruction, warm-up, camera location and operation.

- Students of relatively equal skill — determined by prior assessment — should be paired together.

Safety:

- Area should be mowed and be free of obstructions.

Equipment:

- 8 polyspots or 4-inch cones.

- Lane marked 15 feet x 150 feet.

- Appropriate-size soccer ball.

Diagram of Space/Distance – Mark Camera Location

A=Player A-Starting position   B=Player B-Starting Position
▲=Polyspots mark passing lane (Passing lane=10 ft wide and approximately 60 ft long).
Path of Partner B= ▬▬▬▬▬▬
Path of Ball= - - - - - - - - ►
Path of Partner A= ▬ ▬ ▬
Starting Line= ▬▬▬▬▬

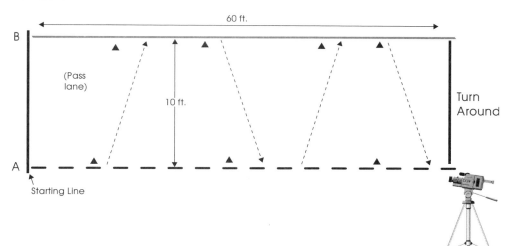

Camera Location/Operation

The camera should be placed to the side of the end line so that the players can be viewed for the entire distance to be traveled. The beginning line should be seen at the top and the end line at the bottom of the viewing screen.

Assessment Score Sheet

PE Teacher _____   Grade _____   Date _____

School _____   Classroom Teacher _____

Student Name	ID Number	Gender	Dribbling (0-4)	Passing (0-4)	Receiving (0-4)	Total Score (0-12) 9=Competent

NASPE

Standard 1:

Demonstrates competence in motor skills and movement patterns needed to perform a variety of physical activities.

Performance Indicator:

Use offensive skills to maintain possession of an object in a 2-on-1 situation.

Assessment Task:

Use offensive skills to maintain possession of the ball in a 2-on-1 game of soccer.

Criteria for Competence (Level 3):

1. Usually moves to create open space and a passing lane.
2. Usually sends a receivable lead pass to a teammate.
3. Usually receives a receivable pass and controls ball.

■ Assessment Rubric:

Level	1. Movement Without the Ball	2. Passing	3. Receiving
4	Consistently moves to create open space and a passing lane.	Consistently sends a receivable lead pass to a teammate.	Consistently receives a receivable pass and controls ball.
3	Usually moves to create open space and a passing lane.	Usually sends a receivable lead pass to a teammate.	Usually receives a receivable pass and controls ball.
2	Sometimes moves to create open space and a passing lane.	Sometimes sends a receivable lead pass to a teammate.	Sometimes receives a receivable pass and controls ball.
1	Seldom moves to create open space and a passing lane.	Seldom sends a receivable lead pass to a teammate.	Seldom receives a receivable pass and controls ball.
0	Violates safety procedures and/or does not complete the assessment task.		

Consistently = 90% and above

Usually = 75% - 89%

Sometimes = 50% - 74%

Seldom = below 50%

■ Assessment Protocols:

Directions for Students (Read aloud, verbatim):

- You and your partner will play a 2-on-1 game of soccer against a defender for 1 minute.
- You will be assessed on your ability to:

  a) move to create open space and passing lanes.

  b) send receivable passes.

  c) receive receivable passes.
- All passes must be leading passes, so that the receiver must move to the ball.
- One partner will start play. Each time play is interrupted, play will be resumed alternating the initiator.

Directions for Teachers:

Preparation

- See the chapter titled Procedures to Administer & Score PE Metrics Assessments for instruction, warm-up, camera location and operation.
- Students of relatively equal skill — determined by prior assessment — should be paired together.
- Select several students to alternate as the defensive player. Instruct defender to moderately restrict, obstruct or intercept passes.
- One partner will start play. Each time play is interrupted, play will be resumed alternating the initiator.

Safety:

- Fields should be mowed short, level and free from holes and obstruction.

Equipment:

- Marked field.
- Soccer ball.
- 4 cones.
- Pinnies/jerseys of a contrasting color.
- Stopwatch.

Diagram of space/distance

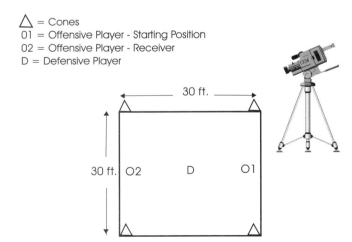

△ = Cones
O1 = Offensive Player - Starting Position
O2 = Offensive Player - Receiver
D = Defensive Player

30 ft.

30 ft. | O2   D   O1

Camera Location/Operation:

The camera should be placed at a corner with sufficient distance to see all boundary lines within the viewing screen.

Assessment Score Sheet

PE Teacher _____   Grade _____   Date _____

School _____   Classroom Teacher _____

Student Name	ID Number	Gender	Movement without the Ball (0-4)	Passing (0-4)	Receiving (0-4)	Total Score (0-12) 9=Competent

5 Grade
Striking With a Paddle

Standard 1:

Demonstrates competency in motor skills and movement patterns needed to perform a variety of physical activities.

Performance Indicator:

Strike an object continuously with a paddle or racquet.

Assessment Task:

Strike a ball against the wall continuously with a short-handled paddle.

Criteria for Competence (Level 3):

1. Usually uses a side orientation.
2. Strikes the ball continuously against the wall 5 times from 10 feet with added strokes that may be in front of the 10-foot striking line.

■ Assessment Rubric:

Level	1. Form	2. Continuous Strikes
4	Consistently uses a side orientation.	Strikes the ball continuously against the wall 5 times in a row from 10 feet with no hits in front of the 10-foot striking line.
3	Usually uses a side orientation.	Strikes the ball continuously against the wall 5 times from 10 feet with added strokes that may be in front of the 10- foot striking line.
2	Sometimes uses a side orientation.	Strikes the ball continuously against the wall at least 4 times from 10 feet with added strokes that may be in front of the 10-foot striking line.
1	Seldom uses a side orientation.	Strikes the ball continuously against the wall fewer than 4 times from 10 feet with added strokes that may be in front of the 10-foot striking line.
0	Violates safety procedures and/or does not complete the assessment task.	

Consistently = 90% and above

Usually = 75% - 89%

Sometimes = 50% -74%

Seldom = below 50%

■ Assessment Protocols:

Directions for Students (Read aloud, verbatim):

- You will strike a ball continuously, using a forehand and/or backhand stroke, against a wall at least 5 times. Your goal is 5 good hits from behind the 10-foot line against the wall, with only 1 bounce each time.
- You will be assessed on your ability to:
  a) use a side orientation.
  b) strike the ball continuously against the wall at least 5 times from behind the 10 foot line with added strokes that may be in front of the 10-foot striking line.
- You may strike the ball in front of the 10-foot striking line but that hit doesn't count as one of your 5 hits.
- Strike the ball after no more than 1 bounce between each contact. If the ball bounces twice, that trial is ended.
- You will have 2 opportunities to make 5 hits against the wall from behind the 10-foot line without a miss. If you do it on the first try, you don't have to do it again.
- Begin each trial by dropping the ball to bounce it prior to hitting it. Your score is counted with the hit following the first rebound from the wall.

Directions for Teachers: Preparation

- See the chapter titled Procedures to Administer & Score PE Metrics Assessments for instruction, warm-up, camera location and operation.
- Trial is ended when the student fails to contact the ball before it bounces a second time, or fails to contact the ball at all. Signal the end of the trial after the 5th strike behind the 10-foot line is completed. (Student may not put his/her whole foot in front of the 10-foot line.)
- Balls contacted in front of the 10-foot striking line are not counted.
- Students are allowed 2 trials.
- Assess 1 student at a time.

Safety:

- Courts are to be dry and free of obstruction, with adequate 10-foot space beyond the 10-foot striking line to permit forward and backward movement as needed.

Equipment:

- Floor tape for marking striking area.
- 2 cones.
- Pickleballs and wooden or plastic paddle.

Diagram of Space/Distance – Mark Camera Location

Assessment may be performed in a gymnasium or on an outdoor court against a backstop. A line 2 inches wide and 15 feet long, is to be placed 10 feet from and parallel to the wall or backstop.

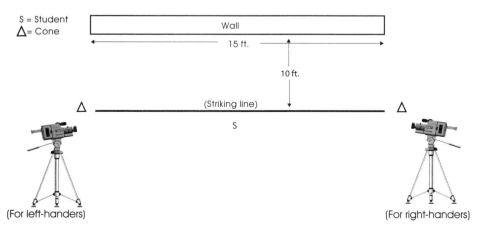

S = Student
△ = Cone

Wall

15 ft.

10 ft.

(Striking line)

S

(For left-handers)   (For right-handers)

Camera Location/Operation:

The camera can be placed to the side and slightly behind the striking line so that the length of the striking line, cones and wall and the student can be seen at the side edge of the viewing screen.

Assessment Score Sheet

PE Teacher _____   Grade _____   Date _____

School _____   Classroom Teacher _____

Student Name	ID Number	Gender	Form (0-4)	Continuous Strikes (0-4)	Total Score (0-8) 6=Competence

Standards 2–6
Performance Descriptors & Sample Questions

This book and the accompanying CD-ROM provide sample assessment questions for National Standards 2-6. The sample questions are divided by performance descriptor so that teachers can select questions based on the content that they've taught their students. Teachers may use entire tests for a standard or may select items across or within particular standards.

PE Metrics: Assessing National Standards 1-6 in Elementary Schools offers the test items in two different ways:

1. The book offers printed sample question items keyed to specific standards and performance descriptors. Teachers may use these items, especially for formative assessments. Note: Correct answers are in bold type.

2. The CD-ROM accompanying this book contains the same sample test items and performance descriptors, and teachers are encouraged to copy them into a Word document from which to administer items to students. Note: Answer keys are at the end of each sample test bank.

Note: NASPE's test-writing committees developed no written assessments for kindergarten students because committee members believe that a written test is not appropriate for that grade level.

Standard 2, Grade 2
Performance Descriptors & Sample Questions

Performance Descriptor: Identifies the critical elements of fundamental locomotor and non-locomotor skills.

Sample Questions

1. When you hop, it means that you start on two feet and land on two feet.
   A. True
   B. False *

2. A jump means that you start on one foot and land on the same foot.
   A. True
   B. False

3. When you slide, you keep the same lead foot as you move sideways.
   A. True
   B. False

4. When galloping, the same foot leads all the time.
   A. True
   B. False

Performance Descriptor: Identifies the movement concepts of body, space, effort and relationships as they relate to fundamental movement skills.

Sample Questions

5. When moving in general space, you should keep as close to other people as you can, without hitting them.
   A. True
   B. False

6. You should run in a zig-zag pathway when you don't want to be tagged.
   A. True
   B. False

7. To do a forward roll, take the weight on your hands and place the top of your head on the mat.
   A. True
   B. False

Performance Descriptor: Identifies the role of practice in improving performance.

Sample Questions

8. If you practice throwing overhand and do it correctly, you can get better at hitting the target.
   A. True
   B. False

*Correct answers are in **bold** type.

9. You don't need to practice dribbling or passing if you are better at it than your friends.
    A. True
    B. False

Performance Descriptor: Identifies ways to increase balance.

Sample Question

10. You have more balance if you are low to the ground compared to standing up higher.
    A. True
    B. False

Performance Descriptor: Identifies reasons why one person might be good at a skill and another person of the same age might not be good at it.

Sample Question

11. You will be a better player than your partner if you are bigger and stronger.
    A. True
    B. False

Performance Descriptor: Identifies the critical elements of fundamental manipulative skills.

Sample Questions

12. You should use your toes to kick a soccer ball.
    A. True
    B. False

13. When catching a ball on the ground with two hands, your fingers should point toward each other.
    A. True
    B. False

14. For a good overhand throw, you should start facing the target.
    A. True
    B. False

15. When dribbling, push the ball downward with a flat hand.
    A. True
    B. False

16. You should keep your arms straight as you catch the ball.
    A. True
    B. False

17. When you toss underhand, you step forward with the same foot as your tossing arm.
    A. True
    B. False

Performance Descriptor: Identifies the movement concepts of body, space, effort and relationships as they relate to fundamental manipulative skills.

Sample Questions

18. If you want to hit a ball harder and farther with a paddle, you should use a bigger backswing.
    A. **True**
    B. False

19. When throwing to someone far away from you, use an underhand throw.
    A. True
    B. **False**

Performance Descriptor: Identifies ways to reduce force.

Sample Question

20. When catching a ball at your waist, reach out with "soft hands" and palms pointing upward and pull it in toward your body.
    A. **True**
    B. False

Performance Descriptor: Describes the similarities and differences between the physical performance of girls and boys at age 10.

Sample Question

21. Girls can learn to throw a ball as well as boys can learn to throw a ball.
    A. **True**
    B. False

Standard 2, Grade 5
Performance Descriptors & Sample Questions

Performance Descriptor: Describes the types of practice that improve performance.

Sample Questions

1. The best way to practice to get better at a skill is to practice:
   A. It does not matter how long you practice.
   B. Every other day for two hours.
   C. Every other day for a little while.
   D. Every day for a little while. *

2. During practice to improve a skill, think about:
   A. How the whole skill is used in a game.
   B. How the rules of the game affect the skill.
   C. Doing each part of the skill correctly.
   D. What you did wrong in the last practice.

3. How can Mary get better at dribbling and then shooting a basketball? She should think about:
   A. How far she should be from the basket.
   B. Where to aim the ball.
   C. How to dribble the ball down the court.
   D. How to change from dribbling to shooting.

4. How can Jamie practice to get better at striking with a bat?
   A. Hit off of a tee until he can hit every ball.
   B. Hit off of a tee at first, then hit soft-toss pitches.
   C. Hit pitches that the pitcher throws.
   D. Start with very fast pitches so that he knows what he needs to learn.

5. Which best describes the kind of practice that will improve skill performance? Practice that is done:
   A. Rarely, but for long times, including thinking about key parts of the skill and making changes as you get better.
   B. Often, for short times, including thinking about key parts of the skill and making changes as you get better.
   C. Rarely, but for long times, including thinking about key parts of the skill and not changing any key parts.
   D. Often, for short times, including thinking about other skills, and keeping the same routine each time.

* Correct answers are in **bold** type.

Performance Descriptor: Describes critical elements of fundamental skill combinations.

Sample Questions

6. The best cues for a soccer receive and pass are:
   A. **Trap, control, kick.**
   B. Trap, kick, pass.
   C. Kick, control, pass.
   D. Trap, pass, control.

7. Cues for a tumbling routine include which of the following?
   A. Move as quickly as you can.
   B. Balance weight on hands and head, then roll forward.
   C. Balance weight and roll forward as fast as you can.
   D. **Still balances and controlled rolls.**

8. Chris asked you to explain how to do a basketball pass and receive. What should you say?
   A. Throw toward your partner's direction and run away from your partner.
   B. **Aim for your partner's chest, then put out your hand to give your partner a target to pass the ball back to you.**
   C. Throw toward your partner's direction, then put out your hand to give your partner a target for a return pass.
   D. Aim for your partner's chest, then stick out your chest for a return pass.

9. Pat asked you to explain how to do a soccer dribble and short pass. What should you say? The last dribble should:
   A. **Be close, then plant the non-kicking foot next to the ball and strike the ball gently.**
   B. Send the ball ahead of you, then plant the non-kicking foot next to the ball and strike the ball with force.
   C. Be close, then plant the non-kicking foot behind the ball and strike with force.
   D. Send the ball ahead of you, then plant the non-kicking foot behind the ball and strike with force.

10. Pat asked you to explain how to receive and then dribble a soccer ball while being guarded closely. What should you say?
    A. Run up to the ball and start kicking it in front of you while you run.
    B. Trap the ball by stepping on it, then tap the ball while dribbling down the field as fast as you can.
    C. **Trap the ball by giving with the foot, then tap the ball gently, keeping it close to your foot while you run.**
    D. Trap the ball, then kick it in front of you as you move down the field.

11. Maria wants to get better at dancing. What can you say to help her? Practice dance steps:
    A. With a partner who is better than her before trying the steps alone.
    B. To her favorite music before trying to get the steps right.
    C. One by one, then add fast music when she puts the steps together the first time.
    D. **Without music first, then move in time to gradually faster music.**

12. Your brother wants to learn to run faster while dribbling a basketball. What can you tell him to help him?

    A. Push the ball farther in front of you and keep your head up.

    B. Spread your fingers apart more and look at the ball.

    C. Keep the ball at your side and run ahead of it.

    D. Push the ball farther in front of you and look at the ball.

13. After you hit a ball to the shortstop, how should you run to first base?

    A. Run fast, then turn toward second base.

    B. Slow down as you get to the base.

    C. Slide into first base.

    D. Touch the base with one foot and run past it.

14. How would you tell Tomas to turn left on his inline skates?

    A. Look left, lean hips to left, push skates left.

    B. Rotate upper body left, look ahead, push skates hard.

    C. Look left, rotate upper body left, lead with left foot.

    D. Lean forward, swing weight out to left, line up skates front to back.

15. How would you tell Anna the difference between passing and shooting in floor hockey?

    A. Move the stick faster for shooting than for passing.

    B. Have your hands farther apart for shooting than for passing.

    C. The puck should be farther away from you for shooting than for passing.

    D. You should be running faster when shooting than when passing.

Performance Descriptor: Describes ways to generate force.

Sample Questions

16. Force can be increased by:

    A. Stepping forward as you throw.

    B. Stepping with the foot on the same side as the throwing hand.

    C. Releasing the ball sooner.

    D. Releasing the ball later.

17. To jump as high as you can from a standing position:

    A. Reach with arms while getting low to the ground.

    B. Start with your body low to the ground.

    C. Swing arms and bend your hips, knees and ankles.

    D. Reach with arms while keeping legs straight.

18. If Johnnie wants to kick a ball far, he should swing his leg back with a:

    A. Bent knee, then swing forward, straightening his leg.

    B. Bent knee, then swing forward, keeping knee bent.

    C. Straight leg, then swing forward, bending knee.

    D. Straight leg, then swing forward, keeping leg straight.

19. When Laura throws a longer distance, which body parts will she use first to help her throw farther?
    A. Throwing arm only.
    B. Legs.
    C. Stomach.
    D. Shoulders.

20. Which of the following is true? Stationary objects need:
    A. The same amount of force to move as moving objects do to move.
    B. Less force to move than moving objects do to move.
    C. More force to move than moving objects do to move.
    D. No force to begin moving.

21. When throwing for distance, use _____ body parts.
    A. Only upper.
    B. Upper and lower.
    C. Only the right side of.
    D. Only lower.

Performance Descriptor: Describes the changes that occur during childhood and puberty, along with their impact on physical performance.

Sample Questions

22. Students younger than age 11 should not lift heavy weights because:
    A. Weights are made for adults.
    B. Children should not develop muscle strength.
    C. Growth plates might be injured.
    D. Children cannot understand the directions for strength exercises.

23. As boys and girls get bigger and stronger, what happens to them? They run:
    A. Longer, get clumsier and kick and throw farther.
    B. Faster and hit targets easier.
    C. Longer, get more flexible and have better balance.
    D. Faster and can kick and throw farther.

Performance Descriptor: Describes how space and relationships are used in basic game strategies.

Sample Questions

24. When working with a partner in 2-v-1 game, Louis should move:
    A. Away from his partner.
    B. Close to his partner.
    C. Close to the defender.
    D. As little as possible.

25. Where should Sam move during a 3-v-3 Ultimate Frisbee® game when her team has the Frisbee®?
    A. To open space.
    B. To the end zone.
    C. Toward the person with the Frisbee®.
    D. Behind the defender.

26. If Lee wants to get open for a pass, he should:
    A. Create space by dodging and cutting.
    B. Move slowly enough for his teammates to see him at all times.
    C. Dodge and cut toward the defenders.
    D. Move toward the goal.

27. If Jeanne has the ball, how can she help her team move the ball toward the goal?   Make passes:
    A. Only toward the goal.
    B. In front of her teammate.
    C. Directly to her teammate.
    D. In front of the defenders.

28. When playing defense, Sheri should:
    A. Stay between the ball and the closest player on the other team.
    B. Stay between the ball and the goal.
    C. Stay very close to her opponent.
    D. Allow the other team to set up in its offense without any pressure.

29. If you are playing offense with a partner who is running toward the goal and is against one defender, how should you pass the ball to your teammate?
    A. Hard, to make the defender miss.
    B. Behind the teammate.
    C. In front of the teammate.
    D. Directly to the teammate.

30. The best way for Liam to get open for a pass, is by:
    A. Keeping the passing lane open between himself and the person with the ball.
    B. Staying close to whoever has the ball.
    C. Trying to stay even with whoever has the ball.
    D. Avoiding moving toward any passes to him so that his defender stays confused.

Standards 3 & 4, Grade 2
Performance Descriptors & Sample Questions

Performance Descriptor: Identifies physical activity in school and outside of school (types, settings & characteristics).

Sample Questions

1. You can play all physical activities by yourself.
   - A) True
   - **B) False***

2. Even if you play soccer during recess, you need more physical activity at home.
   - **A) True**
   - B) False

3. If I am active at school, I do **NOT** have to be active at home to be healthy.
   - A) True
   - **B) False**

4. It is hard to be physically active when your friends and family are not physically active.
   - **A) True**
   - B) False

5. Standing and talking to your friends is a good physical activity.
   - A) True
   - **B) False**

Performance Descriptor: Identifies physiological changes from physical activity.

Sample Questions

6. Sweating means that you are **NOT** playing hard.
   - A) True
   - **B) False**

7. Your heart beats more slowly when you walk than when you run.
   - **A) True**
   - B) False

Performance Descriptor: Identifies different frequencies of physical activity.

Sample Questions

8. You need to play only once a week to be physically fit.
   - A) True
   - **B) False**

*Correct answers are in **bold** type

9. If I am physically active today, I do not need to be active tomorrow.
   A) True
   B) False

10. Daily physical activity can make your muscles hurt too much.
    A) True
    B) False

Performance Descriptor: Identifies the components of health-related fitness.

Sample Questions

11. Chris is physically fit because he brushes his teeth.
    A) True
    B) False

12. Stretching helps you become more flexible.
    A) True
    B) False

13. Muscle strength is part of health-related fitness.
    A) True
    B) False

Performance Descriptor: Identifies the benefits of physical activity for health, weight control, mood & self-esteem.

Sample Questions

14. It is not healthy to play hard every day of the week.
    A) True
    B) False

15. Having stronger muscles helps you throw a ball farther.
    A) True
    B) False

16. Most physical activities are harder for people who are overweight.
    A) True
    B) False

17. Physical activity can help you feel better.
    A) True
    B) False

Performance Descriptor: Identifies different intensities of physical activity.

Sample Questions

18. Playing tag with friends and walking to the bus are both hard vigorous physical activities.
    A) True
    B) False

19. When you are playing hard, you can easily have a conversation with friends.
    A) True
    B) False

20. You can play games for a longer period of time if your heart is strong.
    A) True
    B) False

21. You need to stop physical activity when your heart beats fast.
    A) True
    B) False

22. It is just as hard to walk one mile as it is to run one mile.
    A) True
    B) False

Standards 3 & 4, Grade 5
Performance Descriptors & Sample Questions

Performance Descriptor: Chooses to be physically active outside of school.

Sample Questions

1. The best choice for a vigorous physical activity after school is:
   - A. Shooting baskets.
   - B. Throwing and catching with a friend.
   - **C. Riding a bike. ***
   - D. Going for a long walk.

2. Jane wants to do something after school to help her be good on the soccer team. She should:
   - A. Ride her bike for 30 minutes.
   - B. Play a soccer video game for 30 minutes without stopping.
   - **C. Practice dribbling a soccer ball at a fast pace around the yard for 30 minutes.**
   - D. Play on the trampoline for 30 minutes.

Performance Descriptor: Describes personal responses to physical activity.

Sample Question

3. When you exercise vigorously:
   - A. You start to breathe more slowly.
   - B. Your heart keeps a slow, steady rhythm.
   - C. It is more difficult to find your pulse.
   - **D. You increase your pulse.**

Performance Descriptor: Describes characteristics of health-enhancing physical activity.

Sample Questions

4. Bill likes to run, which is called a/an _____ activity:
   - A. Flexibility.
   - **B. Aerobic.**
   - C. Competitive.
   - D. Sport.

5. Which of the following is the most vigorous activity?
   - A. Playing kickball.
   - **B. Running.**
   - C. Riding a bike.
   - D. Playing softball.

* Correct answers are in **bold** type.

6. Soccer and swimming both require a lot of:
   A. Flexibility.
   B. Muscle strength.
   C. Teamwork.
   D. Aerobic endurance.

7. If Jane can pass a flexibility test, she is more likely to:
   A. Participate in a long-distance race.
   B. Lift a heavy weight.
   C. Do well in gymnastics.
   D. Lift light weights many times.

8. What will best improve your aerobic fitness?
   A. Kickball.
   B. Dodgeball.
   C. Golf.
   D. Soccer.

9. Which of the following is a moderate physical activity?
   A. Running.
   B. Walking briskly.
   C. Inline skating.
   D. Playing soccer.

10. Which of the following is a weight-bearing activity?
    A. Riding your bicycle.
    B. Walking.
    C. Doing curl-ups.
    D. Swimming.

11. Softball is a good:
    A. Flexibility-improving activity.
    B. Vigorous activity.
    C. Weight-bearing activity.
    D. Aerobic activity.

Performance Descriptor: Achieves criterion-referenced standards.

Sample Questions

12. When you measure the distance that you can stretch. you are testing:
    A. Muscle strength.
    B. Flexibility.
    C. Muscle endurance.
    D. Strength in your arms.

13. A good score on a health-related fitness test tells you that:
    A. You can perform skills at a high level.
    B. You are not sick.
    C. You have a healthy level of fitness.
    D. You are an athlete.

Performance Descriptor: Identifies personal health-related weaknesses/strengths.

Sample Questions

14. If you are fit, you:
    A. Are good at many skills,
    B. Are good at running but are not flexible,
    C. Have more choices to be physically active.
    D. Are bigger than everyone else your age.

15. Fitness tests are good because they:
    A. Identify areas of fitness that need improvement.
    B. Identify the fit person in the class.
    C. Tell you what activity that you need to join.
    D. Give you a lot of activity when you take them.

16. Your heart beat creates your pulse, which is best checked at your:
    A. Wrist.
    B. Ankle.
    C. Chest.
    D. Thumb.

Performance Descriptor: Describes how to improve personal fitness.

Sample Questions

17. If you score low on an aerobic endurance test, you should:
    A. Increase the number of push-ups you do.
    B. Increase the amount of time resting.
    C. Participate more in strength-building activities.
    D. Increase the amount of vigorous activity you get.

18. To keep a good body-composition score:
    A. Do stretching exercises every day.
    B. Sleep 8 to 10 hours each day.
    C. Eat and burn the same number of calories every day.
    D. Do push-ups and sit-ups each week.

19. If Juan wants to become more flexible, he should:
    A. Decrease the amount of stretching he does.
    B. Exercise a muscle until it starts to feel tired.
    C. Increase the amount of stretching he does.
    D. Work through the pain stage of an exercise.

20. Which of the following will benefit your heart the most?
    A. Stretching your chest after exercise.
    B. Drinking lots of water.
    C. Eating lots of fruits and vegetables.
    D. Daily physical activity.

Performance Descriptor: Identifies the principles (guidelines) associated with improving physical fitness.

Sample Questions

21. To lift a weight many times, you need:
    A. Muscle endurance.
    B. Aerobic endurance.
    C. Muscle strength.
    D. Cardiovascular endurance.

22. In the fitness test, running a mile is used to determine:
    A. How fast you are.
    B. The fitness of your heart.
    C. The coordination of your legs and arms.
    D. How much effort you can demonstrate.

23. The amount of muscle, bone and fat you have in your body determines your:
    A. Aerobic endurance.
    B. Muscle endurance.
    C. Flexibility.
    D. Body composition.

24. If Sara passes all five components of a health-related fitness test, she should:
    A. Keep the same goals and continue what she is doing.
    B. Set new goals and continue what she is doing.
    C. Set new goals to maintain or improve her fitness level.
    D. Keep the same goals and increase what she is doing.

25. When you want to become stronger, you should:
    A. Overload your muscles.
    B. Make sure that your exercise is aerobic.
    C. Flex your muscles as you watch TV.
    D. Avoid stretching the muscle.

Performance Descriptor: Identifies specific benefits associated with each component of health-related physical fitness.

Sample Questions

26. People who are physically fit:
    A. Are older than others in the class.
    B. Feel better.
    C. Are underweight.
    D. Spend all their time playing.

27. When your muscles get stronger:
    A. You can stretch further.
    B. You get hungry more often.
    C. You will lose weight.
    D. You can throw farther.

28. You should participate in weight-bearing activities because they help:
    A. Strengthen your bones.
    B. Improve your flexibility.
    C. Improve your appetite.
    D. Control how much you weigh.

Standards 5 & 6, Grade 2
Performance Descriptors & Sample Questions

Performance Descriptor: Identifies productive work with self and others (e.g., helping, not interfering with others).

Sample Questions

1. If Chris is struggling to toss the ball to you, tell the teacher that you want a different partner.
   A. True
   B. False*

2. Partners work well together when they take the equipment and play alone.
   A. True
   B. False

3. A person who cooperates and takes turns makes a good teammate.
   A. True
   B. False

4. Teamwork is when everyone works together to do something you could not do alone.
   A. True
   B. False

5. My group shows teamwork when the good players get to play and the others watch.
   A. True
   B. False

6. Joe tries his best at tossing and catching, but he always drops the ball. He should stop practicing.
   A. True
   B. False

Performance Descriptor: Identifies sharing as a way to cooperate with others.

Sample Questions

7. An example of students sharing is when two students invite another student to practice throwing and catching a ball with them.
   A. True
   B. False

8. If there is only one ball available at recess, you should choose a game that has many players and invite your classmates to play.
   A. True
   B. False

* Correct answers are in **bold** type.

Performance Descriptor: Recognizes safe procedures for retrieving, using and returning equipment.

Sample Questions

9. At the end of the class, you should keep practicing as you put the ball away.
   A. True
   B. False

10. When someone's ball comes into your space, you should quickly kick the ball out of your space.
    A. True
    B. False

11. Maria is using equipment safely when she tosses the paddle at her partner to use.
    A. True
    B. False

12. If your paddle is broken, you should stop using it, return it, and ask the teacher for another one.
    A. True
    B. False

Performance Descriptor: Identifies increased enjoyment as a result of gaining competence in movement skills.

Sample Questions

13. New games are more fun if you practice the skills first to get better at them and then learn and play by the rules.
    A. True
    B. False

14. If Caleb is a fast runner, he should sign up to race in a track meet.
    A. True
    B. False

Performance Descriptor: Identifies trying new activities as providing challenge.

Sample Questions

15. Even if you think you might not be good, you should try playing a new game and learn new skills.
    A. True
    B. False

16. When the teacher asks you to try a game you never played before, you should ask if you can sit and watch.
    A. True
    B. False

17. Trying different activities and learning new games can be fun and will help you improve your physical skills.
    A. True
    B. False

18. If your teacher wants you to try a new activity that you think you will not like, you should sit down and refuse to try it.
    A. True
    B. False

19. If you want to learn new activities, choose only those activities with skills that you already know how to do.
    A. True
    B. False

20. You should not try new activities if your friend says it might be hard.
    A. True
    B. False

Performance Descriptor: Identifies physical activity (benefits) as a way to become healthier.

Sample Questions

21. Playing games that make your heart beat fast is good for your health.
    A. True
    B. False

22. Sitting and talking during recess is a better choice than running and playing tag if you want to pay attention when you return to class.
    A. True
    B. False

23. You know you have been playing hard if your body gets warm, you are sweating and your heart beats faster.
    A. True
    B. False

Standards 5 & 6, Grade 5
Performance Descriptors & Sample Questions

Performance Descriptor: Describes appropriate behavior (e.g., show of support & encouragement, including everyone) during cooperative and practice settings.

Sample Questions

1. Mary and Angela are passing a basketball back and forth to see how many chest passes they can make before missing the ball. Mary keeps missing the pass. What should Angela say?
   A. "Am I throwing the ball too hard for you?"
   B. "How can I help you with your catch?"
   C. "Watch the ball go into your hands. You can do it." *
   D. "Keep practicing."

2. How can Murphy best help others create a dance routine?
   A. Create the routine by herself and then give it to them.
   B. Share an old routine that she learned last year.
   C. Encourage them while she watches.
   D. Give ideas for the moves that will begin the routine.

3. Your classmate, Billy, cannot perform the forearm pass successfully in volleyball practice. What can you say to encourage him?
   A. "Billy, maybe you need to practice more."
   B. "You are not very good at this; maybe you need another sport."
   C. "Billy, you are not strong enough. Move closer to the net."
   D. "Keep your arms straight when you hit the ball, Billy; you will get it."

4. How should Bill respond when the teacher asks him to work with a new student?
   A. Arrange to have the new student participate with someone else who does not have a partner.
   B. Quietly tell the teacher he has already chosen a partner and suggest someone else for the new student.
   C. Ask the new student to be his partner.
   D. Ask his best friend to be his partner.

5. When playing at recess, how should you respond when someone gives you suggestions on how to improve your play?
   A. Switch to play a different game.
   B. Try the suggestions and see if your play improves.
   C. Watch others to see if they try the suggestions.
   D. Ask the person to show you.

* Correct answers are in **bold** type.

Performance Descriptor: Describes appropriate behavior (e.g., not blaming others) during competitive settings.

Sample Questions

6. Which of these actions is the best example of self-control after a disagreement during a game?
   A. Continue to play while staying calm.
   B. Sit out of the game until you are calm.
   C. Avoid talking to other players.
   D. Calmly ask the teacher to put you in a different game.

7. Which is the best way to deal with losing an Ultimate Frisbee® game?
   A. Explain to your teammates everything they did wrong.
   B. Ask the teacher if you can switch teams for the next game.
   C. Tell your teammates that you are tired of losing and they need to try harder.
   D. Congratulate the winning team and work to play better next time.

8. When Yolanda gets angry with at her friend Lois while practicing a jump-rope routine, how should she react?
   A. Ask the teacher to help her with the problem.
   B. Calmly walk away from Lois and not find another activity.
   C. Tell Lois why she is angry.
   D. Calmly ask Lois to discuss the problem and settle the disagreement.

9. Juanita has been reminded by her teammate to play within the sidelines. In response, Juanita should:
   A. Move in bounds quickly.
   B. Stop playing the game.
   C. Say that she did not go out of bounds.
   D. Say that someone else went out of bounds, too.

10. Tony is playing goalie and misses the ball, allowing the other team to score. Tony's teammates should:
    A. Tell Tony that he made a good attempt and encourage him to keep playing hard.
    B. Tell Tony that he needs to play a different position if he wants to help the team.
    C. Wait until after the game is over, then tell Tommy he needs to practice.
    D. Ask another teammate to play goalie and ask Tony to change positions.

11. Ronnie struck out the last time he was at bat. It would be best to:
    A. Tell him to watch the ball and not swing too hard.
    B. Give him encouragement and support him the next time he is at bat.
    C. Make him the last batter.
    D. Tell him to watch a few pitches before swinging.

12. While playing paddle ball, Keisha says the ball landed out of bounds, but Raymond says it was in bounds. What should they do?
    A. Ask a classmate.
    B. Replay the point.
    C. Let the player closer to the ball decide.
    D. Ask the teacher how to decide.

Performance Descriptor: Describes behaviors that contribute to group success.

Sample Questions

13. When working with a group to achieve a goal, it is most important to:
    A. Give the group leader responsibility to make the decisions.
    B. Include everyone in the group in reaching the goal.
    C. Achieve the goal as quickly as possible.
    D. Let the best-skilled people decide how to reach the goal.

14. Lance is working with four teammates to see how long they can keep a volleyball in the air using forearm and overhead passes. What would you suggest to help them be successful as a team?
    A. Everyone needs to talk to each other.
    B. Stop to watch others when they miss the ball.
    C. Watch to see what teammates do.
    D. Try to send the ball to the best players.

15. How can a player best add to the efforts of a hockey team?
    A. Pass to the best player as soon as you get the ball/puck.
    B. Shoot for the goal every time you get the ball/puck.
    C. Work with other teammates to score.
    D. Focus only on scoring goals for the team.

16. How can Gina help her group performance when she already knows the dance?
    A. Practice with the least-skilled member of the group while the others watch.
    B. Demonstrate the dance while the others sit and watch.
    C. Continue to practice so that she does not forget.
    D. Help others in her group learn to perform the routine.

17. When working with a team to complete a challenge successfully, you should:
    A. Come up with an idea quickly and tell them to use it.
    B. Tell them to use the first solution anyone suggests.
    C. Make sure that everyone participates in completing the challenge.
    D. Have the team members who do not have any ideas sit and watch.

Performance Descriptor: Describes how to cooperate with more-skilled and less-skilled participants.

Sample Questions

18. How should Leroy respond to a student who is still learning how to play the game?
    A. Offer to help the student during recess.
    B. Ask the student to sit out and watch until ready to play.
    C. Suggest that the student practice parts of the game that are difficult.
    D. Tell the student what to do during the game.

19. Carlos is the best basketball player in the class. The teacher has asked you to play Carlos in a game of 1-on-1 basketball. You should:
   A. Ask Carlos to help you with your skills instead of playing a game.
   B. Play your best and, at the end of the game, tell him that he plays well.
   C. Ask the teacher to pair you with someone else.
   D. Tell Carlos that he might not want to play with you, because he is much better than you.

20. Bethany is competing in a 3-on-3 soccer game and every time her teammate, Nigel, gets the ball, the other team steals it from him. What should she do the next time Nigel gets the ball?
   A. Tell him to dribble the ball faster.
   B. Tell him to pass the ball to her as soon as he gets it.
   C. Encourage him by making suggestions for getting by the defender.
   D. Move to an open space and call for the ball.

21. John is not very skilled at basketball and gets nervous when he has to dribble the ball during an activity. Tommy knows that John feels uncomfortable. Tommy should:
   A. Not talk to John while he is trying to dribble.
   B. Give John words of encouragement and a few pointers.
   C. Help John while others are watching.
   D. Tell him to practice more during recess.

22. Gina enjoys long-rope jumping. She sees that Sally is having trouble turning a long jump rope. What should Gina do?
   A. Show Sally how to hold and turn the rope correctly.
   B. Suggest that Sally practice after school.
   C. Encourage Sally to figure it out for herself.
   D. Find someone who can help Sally.

Performance Descriptor: Recognizes opportunities for physical activity outside of class.

Sample Questions

23. You learn how to play tennis in physical education class and really like it. How can you continue to improve your skills?
   A. Practice using a tennis video game.
   B. Read about tennis in the newspaper or online.
   C. Join a recreation tennis program in your community.
   D. Hope to play tennis with your friends.

24. Which of the following best describes a student who is most physically active outside of physical education class? Someone who:
   A. Plays baseball on the weekends.
   B. Works hard during every physical education class.
   C. Rides a bike at least once a week.
   D. Participates in at least 60 minutes of physical activity per day.

25. The best place to look to participate in physical activities would be:
    A. At a recreation center in the next town.
    B. At school during recess.
    C. At a gym that you pay to join.
    D. In a location that is close to home.

26. Charlie and his three friends are looking for something to do Saturday afternoon. Which of the following would be the best choice for physical activity?
    A. Play a game of 2-on-2 basketball.
    B. Practice working on skills.
    C. Go to a basketball game.
    D. Play a game of 1-on-1 basketball.

Performance Descriptor: Recognizes the benefits of participation in physical activity, such as physical activity as a positive opportunity for group/peer interaction, challenge, practice and improving skills.

Sample Questions

27. Jeremy is often chosen last during recess to be on a basketball team and wants to improve his skills. Jeremy should:
    A. Use physical activity time to practice basketball skills.
    B. Ask a skilled player to tell him why he is chosen last.
    C. Watch a basketball video to get ideas for improving his skills.
    D. Play basketball with less-skilled players.

28. Kyle enjoys physical activities that are challenging. He likely would not enjoy:
    A. Playing with less-skilled players.
    B. Playing games instead of practicing.
    C. Playing with more skilled players.
    D. Playing with younger players.

29. Which of the following is not a reason for participating in physical activity?
    A. To improve skills.
    B. To increase stress.
    C. For challenge.
    D. For enjoyment.

30. When will Laura have the best opportunity to interact with her friends?
    A. Doing her homework.
    B. Going to the library.
    C. Playing a game of soccer.
    D. Playing a video game.

eferences

Ayers, S. (2004). *Ask-PE.* Reston, VA: National Association for Sport and Physical Education.

Corbin, C.B. & Lindsay, R. (2005) *Fitness for life*, (5th ed.). Champaign, IL: Human Kinetics.

Fronske, H. (2007). *Teaching cues for sport skills for secondary school students* (4th ed.). Boston: Cummings.

Graham, G., Holt-Hale, S. & Parker, M. (2010). *Children moving: A reflective approach to teaching physical education* (8th ed.). New York: McGraw Hill.

Grineski, S. (1996). *Cooperative learning in physical education.* Champaign, IL: Human Kinetics.

Hambleton, R.K., Swaminathan, H. & Rogers, J.H. (1991). *Fundamentals of item response theory.* Newbury Park, CA: Sage.

Hastie, P. (2003). *Teaching for lifetime physical activity through quality high school physical education.* Boston, MA: Benjamin Cummings.

Hellison, D. (1995). *Teaching responsibility through physical activity.* Champaign, IL: Human Kinetics.

Kolen, M.J. & Brennan, R.L. (2004). *Test equating, scaling, and linking: Methods and practices* (2nd ed.). New York: Springer.

Lund, J. & Tannehill, D. (2005). *Standards-based physical education curriculum development.* Boston, MA: Jones and Bartlett.

McGee, R. & Farrow, A. (1987). *Test questions for physical education activities.* Champaign, IL: Human Kinetics.

Mohnsen, B. (2003). *Concepts and principles of physical education: What every student needs to know* (2nd ed.). Reston, VA: National Association for Sport and Physical Education.

National Association for Sport and Physical Education. (1995). *Moving into the future: National standards for physical education: A guide to content and assessment.* Reston, VA: Author.

National Association for Sport and Physical Education. (2004). *Moving into the future: National standards for physical education* (2nd ed.). Reston, VA: Author.

National Association for Sport and Physical Education. (2005). *Physical education for lifelong fitness: The Physical Best teacher's guide* (2nd ed.). Champaign, IL: Human Kinetics.

National Association for Sport and Physical Education. (2009). *Appropriate instructional practice guidelines for elementary school physical education.* Reston, VA: Author.

National Association for Sport and Physical Education. (2009). *Appropriate instructional practice guidelines for middle school physical education.* Reston, VA: Author.

National Association for Sport and Physical Education. (2009). *Appropriate instructional practice guidelines for high school physical education.* Reston, VA: Author.

O'Sullivan, M., & Henninger, M. (2000). *Assessment series K-12 physical education: Assessing student responsibility and teamwork*. Reston, VA: National Association for Sport and Physical Education.

Rainey, D.L., Murray, T. D. (2005). *Foundations of personal fitness*. Woodland Hills, CA: Glencoe/McGraw Hill.

Safrit, M.J., Zhu, W., Costa, M.G., & Zhang, L. (1992). The difficulty of sit-up tests: An empirical investigation. *Research Quarterly for Exercise and Sport, 63*(3), 277-283.

Siedentop, D., Hastie, P. & Van Der Mars, H. (2004). *Complete guide to sport education*. Champaign, IL: Human Kinetics.

Silverman, S. & Ennis, C. (Eds.). (2003). *Student learning in physical education* (2nd ed.). Champaign, IL: Human Kinetics.

Spray, J.A. (1987). Recent developments in measurement and possible applications to the measurement of psychomotor behavior. *Research Quarterly for Exercise and Sport, 58*, 203-209.

Steffen, J. & Grosse, S. (2003). *Assessment series K-12 physical education: Assessment in outdoor adventure physical education*. Reston, VA: National Association for Sport and Physical Education.

Umar, J. (1997). Item banking. In J.P. Keeves (Ed.), *Educational research, methodology, and measurement: An international handbook* (2nd ed., pp. 923-930). New York: Elsevier Science.

Zhu, W. (1996). Should total scores from a rating scale be directly used? *Research Quarterly for Exercise and Sport, 67*(3), 363-372.

Zhu, W. (1998). Test equating: What, why, how? *Research Quarterly for Exercise and Sport, 69*, 11-23.

Zhu, W. (2001). An empirical investigation of Rasch equating of motor function tasks. *Adapted Physical Activity Quarterly, 18*(1), 72-89.

Zhu, W. (2006). Constructing tests using item response theory. In T. Wood and W. Zhu (Eds.), *Measurement Theory and Practice in Kinesiology*. pp. 53-76. Champaign, IL: Human Kinetics.

Zhu, W., & Cole, E.L. (1996). Many-faceted Rasch calibration of a gross-motor instrument. *Research Quarterly for Exercise and Sport, 67*(1), 24-34.

Zhu, W. & Safrit, M.J. (1993). The calibration of a sit-ups task using the Rasch Poisson Counts model. *The Canadian Journal of Applied Physiology, 18*(2), 207-219.

Dance References

Listed below are just a few samples of available materials to help teachers choose and teach dances appropriate for elementary grades.

Books

Bennett, J., & Riemer, P. (2006). *Rhythmic activities and dance* (2nd ed). Champaign, IL: Human Kinetics Publishers.

Cone, T., & Cone, S. (2006). *Teaching children dance* (2nd ed). Champaign, IL: Human Kinetics Publishers.

Mehrhof, J., & Parris, P. (2002). *And the beat goes on: Rhythmic activities for K-8.* Emporia, KS: Mirror Publishing Company.

National Association for Sport and Physical Education & National Dance Association (2007). *Teaching Dance in Elementary Physical Education.* Reston, VA: Author.

National Association for Sport and Physical Education & National Dance Association (2007). *Teaching Dance in K-12 Physical Education.* Reston, VA: Author.

Weikart, P.S. (1989). *Teaching movement and dance: A sequential approach to rhythmic movement* (3rd ed). Ypsilanti, MI: High/Scope Press.

Compact discs available from Educational Record Center (www.erckids.com).

Best Dance Collection for Beginners

Best No-Partner Dance Collections

Christy Lane's How-To CD set (includes square, Latin-American and African-Caribbean dances)

 ppendix B

NASPE's National Standards for Physical Education and Elementary-Level Performance Indicators and Assessment Tasks

Standard 1:
Demonstrates competency in motor skills and movement patterns needed to perform a variety of physical activities.

Kindergarten

Performance Indicator:

Throw, catch, dribble, kick and strike from a stationary position.

Assessment Task:

Dribble a ball continuously for 15 seconds with one hand.

Assessment Task:

Strike a balloon continuously with a short-handled paddle, using an underhand pattern, for 20 seconds.

Assessment Task:

Catch a ball tossed by a teacher, using an underhand catching pattern.

Assessment Task:

Use an underhand throwing pattern to send a ball forward through the air to a large target.

Performance Indicator:

Demonstrate hopping, jumping, galloping and sliding.

Assessment Task:

Hop in place.

Assessment Task:

Slide continuously for 30 feet with the preferred foot leading.

Performance Indicator:

Demonstrate a mature pattern of running.

Assessment Task:

Run continuously for 60 feet.

Performance Indicator:

Transfer weight hands/feet.

Assessment Task:

Place weight on the hands and transfer feet sideways over a raised bar and back to the starting position.

Grade 2

Performance Indicator:

Dribble, kick, throw, catch and strike a ball.

Assessment Task:

Approach a stationary ball at a jog and kick with enough force to send it a distance of 30 feet on a smooth, level surface.

Assessment Task:

Dribble a ball with one hand to a cone and back while jogging slowly.

Assessment Task:

Catch a ball tossed by the teacher, using an overhand catching pattern.

Assessment Task:

Strike a ball upward 5 times consecutively with a short-handled paddle.

Performance Indicator:

Perform dance sequences to music.

Assessment Task:

Perform to music a grade-level-appropriate individual or partner dance that uses 3 different patterns.

Performance Indicator:

Demonstrates a mature pattern of jumping, galloping, sliding and skipping.

Assessment Task:

Gallop continuously for 30 feet with one foot leading. Repeat the task with the other foot leading.

Assessment Task:

Jump forward using a two-foot take-off and a two-foot landing.

Assessment Task:

Perform a sequence of 3 locomotor movements (hop, jump, gallop, slide, skip) with smooth transitions between each locomotor movement.

Assessment Task:

Skip continuously for 30 feet.

Performance Indicator:

Create and perform a gymnastics sequence.

Assessment Task:

Combine balancing, transferring weight and rolling actions into a sequence.

Performance Indicator:

Jump and land in various combinations (one to same foot, one to the other foot, one to two feet, two to two feet, two to one foot).

Assessment Task:

From a walk or jog, jump onto a box with a 1-foot take-off, landing on 2 feet, and jump down from the box using a 2-foot take-off and landing on 2 feet.

Grade 5

Performance Indicator:

Use defensive skills to gain possession of an object in a 2-on-1 situation.

Assessment Task:

Gain possession of a basketball in a 2-on-1 situation.

Performance Indicator:

Dribble, pass and receive a ball with a partner.

Assessment Task:

Dribble, pass and receive a basketball while traveling at a jog.

Assessment Task:

Dribble, pass and receive a soccer ball while traveling at a jog.

Performance Indicator:

Use offensive skills to maintain possession of an object in a 2-on-1 situation.

Assessment Task:

Maintain possession of a basketball in 2-on-1 situation.

Assessment Task:

Use offensive skills to maintain possession of the ball in a 2-on-1 game of soccer.

Performance Indicator:

Perform a dance.

Assessment Task:

Perform the given steps and sequences to the beat of the music for an age-appropriate dance (e.g., line, square, folk, step, social).

Performance Indicator:

Dribble and shoot an object for a goal.

Assessment Task:

While jogging, dribble a puck continuously with a hockey stick through a zig-zag obstacle course, and shoot for a goal.

Performance Indicator:

Perform a gymnastics/movement sequence.

Assessment Task:

Perform a self-designed gymnastics/movement sequence with the following 7 components: (1) a starting shape, (2) roll, (3) transfer of weight from feet to hands, (4) balance, (5) leap or jump, (6) turn and (7) ending shape.

Performance Indicator:

Perform sport-specific skills for participation in individual non-competitive activities.

Assessment Task:

Inline skate on a level surface, with changes in direction.

Performance Indicator:

Dribble, kick, throw, catch and strike a ball.

Assessment Task:

Use an overhand throwing pattern to send a ball to a large wall target.

Performance Indicator:

Strike an object continuously with a paddle or racquet.

Assessment Task:

Strike a ball against the wall continuously with a short-handled paddle.

Standard 2

Grade 2

Performance Descriptor:

Identifies the critical elements of fundamental locomotor and non-locomotor skills.

Performance Descriptor:

Identifies the movement concepts of body, space, effort and relationships as they relate to fundamental movement skills.

Performance Descriptor:

Identifies the role of practice in improving performance.

Performance Descriptor:

Identifies ways to increase balance.

Performance Descriptor:

Identifies reasons why one person might be good at a skill and another person of the same age might not be good at it.

Performance Descriptor:

Identifies the critical elements of fundamental manipulative skills.

Performance Descriptor:

Identifies the movement concepts of body, space, effort and relationships as they relate to fundamental manipulative skills.

Performance Descriptor:

Identifies ways to reduce force.

Performance Descriptor:

Describes the similarities and differences between the physical performance of girls and boys at age 10.

Grade 5

Performance Descriptor:

Describes the types of practice that improve performance.

Performance Descriptor:

Describes critical elements of fundamental skill combinations.

Performance Descriptor:

Describes ways to generate force.

Performance Descriptor:

Describes the changes that occur during childhood and puberty, along with their impact on physical performance.

Performance Descriptor:

Describes how space and relationships are used in basic game strategies.

Standards 3 & 4

Grade 2

Performance Descriptor:

Identifies physical activity in school and outside of school (types, settings & characteristics).

Performance Descriptor:

Identifies physiological changes from physical activity.

Performance Descriptor:

Identifies different frequencies of physical activity.

Performance Descriptor:

Identifies the components of health-related fitness.

Performance Descriptor:

Identifies the benefits of physical activity for health, weight control, mood & self-esteem.

Performance Descriptor:

Identifies different intensities of physical activity.

Grade 5

Performance Descriptor:

Chooses to be physically active outside of school.

Performance Descriptor:

Describes personal responses to physical activity.

Performance Descriptor:

Describes characteristics of health-enhancing physical activity.

Performance Descriptor:

Achieves criterion-referenced standards.

Performance Descriptor:

Identifies personal health-related weaknesses/strengths.

Performance Descriptor:

Describes how to improve personal fitness.

Performance Descriptor:

Identifies the principles (guidelines) associated with improving physical fitness.

Performance Descriptor:

Identifies specific benefits associated with each component of health-related physical fitness.

Standards 5 & 6

Grade 2

Performance Descriptor:

Identifies productive work with self and others (e.g., helping, not interfering with others).

Performance Descriptor:

Identifies sharing as a way to cooperate with others.

Performance Descriptor:

Recognizes safe procedures for retrieving, using and returning equipment.

Performance Descriptor:

Identifies increased enjoyment as a result of gaining competence in movement skills.

Performance Descriptor:

Identifies trying new activities as providing challenge.

Performance Descriptor:

Identifies physical activity (benefits) as a way to become healthier.

Grade 5

Performance Descriptor:

Describes appropriate behavior (e.g., show of support & encouragement, including everyone) during cooperative and practice settings.

Performance Descriptor:

Describes appropriate behavior (e.g., not blaming others) during competitive settings.

Performance Descriptor:

Describes behaviors that contribute to group success.

Performance Descriptor:

Describes how to cooperate with more-skilled and less-skilled participants.

Performance Descriptor:

Recognizes opportunities for physical activity outside of class.

Performance Descriptor:

Recognizes the benefits of participation in physical activity, such as physical activity as a positive opportunity for group/peer interaction, challenge, practice and improving skills.

Resources

Published by the National Association for Sport and Physical Education:

Quality Physical Education Programs

- *Concepts and Principles of Physical Education: What Every Student Should Know* (2010)
- *Physical Activity and Sport for the Secondary School Student, 6th Edition* (2010)
- *Moving Into the Future: National Standards for Physical Education, 2nd Edition* (2004)
- *National Standards & Guidelines for Physical Education Teacher Education* (2009)
- *Quality Coaches, Quality Sports: National Standards for Athletic Coaches* (2006)
- *Physical Activity for Children: A Statement of Guidelines for Children Ages 5-12, 2nd Edition* (2003)
- *On Your Mark, Get Set, Go!: A Guide for Beginning Physical Education Teachers* (2004)
- *Coaching Issues & Dilemmas: Character Building Through Sport Participation* (2003)
- *Teaching Games for Understanding in Physical Education and Sport* (2003)

Opportunity to Learn Standards

- *Opportunity to Learn Guidelines for Elementary School Physical Education* (2009)
- *Opportunity to Learn Guidelines for Middle School Physical Education* (2009)
- *Opportunity to Learn Guidelines for High School Physical Education* (2009)

Appropriate Practices

- *Appropriate Practices in Movement Programs for Children Ages 3-5* (2009)
- *Appropriate Instructional Practice Guidelines for Elementary School Physical Education* (2009)
- *Appropriate Instructional Practice Guidelines for Middle School Physical Education* (2009)
- *Appropriate Instructional Practice Guidelines for High School Physical Education* (2009)
- *Appropriate Instructional Practice Guidelines for Higher Education Physical Activity Programs* (2009)

Assessment Series

- *Assessing and Improving Fitness in Elementary Physical Education* (2008)
- *Assessing Concepts: Secondary Biomechanics* (2004)
- *Assessing Student Outcomes in Sport Education* (2003)
- *Assessment in Outdoor Adventure Physical Education* (2003)
- *Assessing Heart Rate in Physical Education* (2002)
- *Authentic Assessment of Physical Activity for High School Students* (2002)
- *Elementary Heart Health: Lessons and Assessment* (2001)
- *Creating Rubrics for Physical Education* (2000)
- *Standards-Based Assessment of Student Learning: A comprehensive Approach* (1999)

Order online at www.naspeinfo.org or call (800) 321-0789

National Association for Sport and Physical Education

an association of the American Alliance for Health, Physical Education, Recreation and Dance

1900 Association Drive • Reston, Va. 20191

703-476-3410 • 703-476-8316 (fax) • www.naspeinfo.org

Notes